How *not* to lose $1 million

How *not* to lose $1 million

Win at investing by losing less

John Addis

Co-founder of Intelligent Investor

MAJOR
STREET

MAJOR STREET

First published in 2024 by Major Street Publishing Pty Ltd
info@majorstreet.com.au | majorstreet.com.au

© John Addis 2024
The moral rights of the author have been asserted.

A catalogue record for this book is available from the National Library of Australia

A catalogue record for this book is available from the National Library of Australia.

Printed book ISBN: 978-1-923186-03-3
Ebook ISBN: 978-1-923186-04-0

Cover design by Typography Studio
Internal design by Production Works

10 9 8 7 6 5 4 3 2 1

Contents

Introduction

How to make better mistakes

I didn't set out to have a career in finance. In fact, I didn't set out to have a career at all, but by the mid-1990s, after studying economics and running fantasy football competitions, I stumbled into advertising. Words were my thing and freelance copywriting felt like a fit. If you recall newspaper ads for home equity loans or Nokia mobile phones from that era, it was probably me. Sorry about that.

Around that time, an investment analyst friend handed me a copy of the publication he worked for. It produced weekly company research on what stocks to buy and sell. I love reading about businesses and the people that run them, but this wasn't what I expected. Full of industry jargon, typos and acronyms, I found it impenetrable. The technical work was okay – the facts, the data, et cetera – but there was no life, no story. This, I later realised, is a hallmark of the finance industry and the first red flag you'll encounter – it is easier to charge a fat fee by overcomplicating things.

In *The Doctor's Dilemma*, Irish playwright George Bernard Shaw wrote that 'all professions are a conspiracy against the laity'. Dense phrases, noxious jargon and a pseudoscientific tone are their tools. In finance, endemic usage blinds those deploying them to their implied purpose: to make clients feel they cannot possibly do this stuff themselves. My friend and I felt there was a better way.

The *Intelligent Investor* began with some baseline principles: we would not talk down to people, we would try to make company research and stock recommendations interesting and profitable, and, through education, we would give members the confidence to build and control their own portfolios. The goal was ambitious, more so when set by a copywriter and a former Kiwi farmer: to beat professional money managers at their own game, thus sparing readers the gruesome alternatives of excessive fees, mediocre performance and dire text.

In March 1998, the first issue arrived at our Bondi Junction office. Inside was our first-ever buy recommendation – the rapidly expanding travel agent Flight Centre. With exceptional owner managers and a wonderful incentive program, it was rolling out bright red stores across the English-speaking world. At $3 a share, we thought the price a bargain, and so it proved. The company eventually became our first ten bagger – a stock that rises 1000 percent – and was emblematic of an approach that would take hold in the years to come, which it is worth taking a few moments to explain.

Value investors aim to buy stocks at a price below their estimate of value. Doing so offers what is called a 'margin of safety'. For example, if you pay $20,000 for a second-hand car you think is worth $30,000, your margin of safety is $10,000, or 33 percent. It's an insurance policy of sorts. Even if your estimate of value is wrong by half, you still make $5,000. If correct, the margin of safety is the source of a $10,000 profit.

To put it another way, value investors like to serve their oblivious dinner guests Aldi rib eye and, when asked if it was purchased at the local gourmet butcher, are disarmingly noncommittal. Value investing is a bargain hunt.

Warren Buffett, a steak fan of some notoriety, is value investing's richest and most famous proponent. Adept at explaining the approach and why so few people successfully pursue it, I felt an immediate attraction. As you shall see, a contrary approach is critical.

No matter your flavour of approach, investing in shares is a good thing. Over time, shares tend to rise faster than any other asset class (property, bonds, cash et cetera). In the 30 years to June 2023, they have outperformed all other major asset classes (see Figure 1).

Figure 1: Market returns from 1 July 1993 to 30 June 2023

It has been this way for a century or more. Building a nest egg for the future, planning for your retirement, or just getting rich slowly is best done through shares.

Once convinced of that argument, you have three choices. The first is to follow Vanguard's preference and buy a portfolio of low-cost index or exchange-traded funds (ETFs). Ideally, you would make monthly additions to your investment and commit to not selling, especially when you most felt like it. If you have no interest in managing your own money, stop reading now. Put the book down and start work on building a portfolio of low-cost index funds or ETFs.

Your second possibility is to pay someone to manage your money to beat the returns offered in option one. In the lingua franca of investing, this is known as 'outperforming the index'. So-called active managers (us included) are ten a penny, but only about a quarter outperform. The remainder tend to produce average returns, minus the fees they charge. Data bears this out: of the Australian fund managers attempting to beat an index over the ten-year period to December 2023, three quarters failed, and the average underperformance was equal to the average annual fee of 1.37 percent.

Fund managers are like drivers. Despite all evidence and the mathematical impossibility of it, most believe they are above average. Setting out to manage money is like getting married – you wouldn't do it if you believed the averages applied to you.

This returns us to the first option: accept that it is better to pay a low price for an average return and forget about trying to beat the index. Fees are manageable in the way that returns are not, and, as Figure 2 shows, there is a huge compounding advantage to doing so.

Figure 2: Fees on $100,000 over 30 years

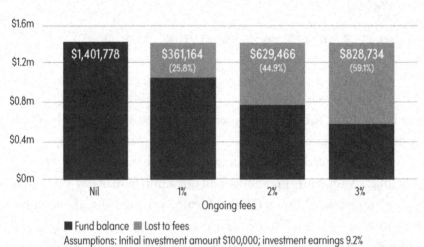

Assumptions: Initial investment amount $100,000; investment earnings 9.2%

The third option results from the first two. It is a generalisation but nevertheless true: the finance sector trades on complexity, preying on the general misunderstanding of the effects of percentages and compounding to enrich those within it at the expense of the clients it is supposed to serve. Investors have cottoned on, and more are doing it for themselves. If you are one of them, this book is for you.

Having made the general case for shares and controlling your own portfolio, let's turn to the particular – the best way of getting higher-than-average returns.

Since 2001, *Intelligent Investor* has been running model income and growth portfolios. Had you invested $10,000 in each of the index, the income portfolio and the growth portfolio in 2001, the index would have returned $60,298 by April 2024, the income portfolio $76,078 and the growth portfolio $145,303.

Beating the index over two decades is unusual but, like monkeys and their typewriters, eventually a bonobo will write *Romeo and Juliet*. We might have been lucky, although as more time passes that possibility falls. Either way, I want to be clear – there is nothing special about me or anyone else involved in *Intelligent Investor*.

I'm a former copywriter with no finance qualifications or any inclination to obtain any, our portfolio manager played AFL at a high level and is currently studying Guns N' Roses guitar solos, and our research director was once a water economist in the public service. We didn't go to fancy universities, get scholarships or academically excel – at least, not in my case. The same could be said of other analytical team members. We are not the secret sauce.

What has made a difference is the application of value investing principles and their refinement over the decades. Disciplined by the public display and self-analysis or our errors, we and our members improved without being waylaid by short-term performance bonuses.

You have the same advantages, with one caveat: that you enjoy investing and are comfortable with making mistakes and losing money. If you are unsure, this book will help you decide if it is right for you.

The path to investing success is one of repetitive failure. Mistakes are like the sun and the daylight: without one, there is no other. The learning is in the failing.

Odd, then, that investing books rarely cover failures. The reasons are as obvious as they are nefarious. No fund manager charging a hefty fee wants to look foolish in public. The mystery and conspiracy must be maintained. This defies a greater truth: to learn something new of any significance requires a willingness to look foolish.

I consider a willingness to look stupid one of our competitive advantages. This book aims to strengthen it. Publicly exposing and analysing our mistakes before members has made both parties better investors. This book will do the same for you. Having lost well over $1 million through my own investing errors, I feel well qualified to write it.

There are other, more practical reasons for making better mistakes than simply chasing big winners. First, it improves returns. Avoiding a big loser is as useful as picking a big winner – more so, in fact. Avoiding a stock that tumbles 70 percent means you don't have to find one or more stocks that rise by a similar amount.

Studying investments on which you or someone else has lost money is more likely to help you pick big winners because we learn more from doing things wrong than right. The shadow is what helps us see the light. Studying our losers will help you to identify high-quality companies and spot the red flags that send investments off the rails.

Finally, reducing your losses also reduces stress. When investors mention their sleepless nights, it isn't due to stocks rising too quickly or not going anywhere at all. Those that are crashing do the damage. Each case study in this book concerns a sleepless-night stock. By learning through our experience, you should sleep better and become a better, more successful investor.

The book is divided into four parts, each concerning a particular category of error. The first addresses the stocks we watched go off course but acted on too late. This is probably the most common kind of error and one new investors are most likely to make.

The second covers the most financially damaging category of error: selling high-quality, fast-growing businesses too soon. You will recognise the companies and be stunned by the lost gains.

The third is a class of error common to value investors: stocks that we thought looked cheap but shouldn't have bought at all. The phrase to describe such situations is 'catching a falling knife'. The cuts were deep, painful and illuminating.

The final category is a little different: the stocks we researched, liked and maybe should have bought but didn't. Not buying attractive stocks that you should is part and parcel of investing. The first case study, covering Meta, is about learning to let these situations go. It is followed by a stock we never considered buying – buy-now-pay-later company Afterpay – as a means of showing the dangers of seeking huge winners.

The case studies are supported by a collection of essays in the Appendix that flesh out some of the issues raised. It should also be noted that whilst most of the case studies relate to mistakes by *Intelligent Investor* (us), a few focus on my personal errors (I).

The book has been written for investors who want to improve their skills and those thinking about managing their own money. I've tried to avoid jargon and industry terms, explaining them where required. If there are terms you don't understand, please refer to the Glossary.

References relate mainly to *Intelligent Investor* research. These are listed at the end of each case study. Where references are made to external sources, these are footnoted.

Lastly, the book is written for you to dip in and out of. Start where you want and go where you want – it doesn't matter. Every section and case study will help you make better mistakes.

Part I
Stocks We Sold
Too Late

In her book *Quit: The Power of Knowing When to Walk Away*, Annie Duke tells the story of Muhammad Ali's rise against the odds to become the greatest boxer of all time. Refusing to serve in the Vietnam War, Ali was stripped of his heavyweight title in 1967.

Unable to box for three and a half years, it took him four more years before he could challenge George Foreman to regain the title. In 1974, aged 33 and a decade after originally being crowned champion, that is what he achieved. This tremendous sporting feat is still celebrated today, along with the grit and unbreakable determination that helped bring it about.

When he regained the title, Ali had competed in 46 professional fights. Despite signs of mental and physical deterioration, and warnings from doctors and advisers, he went on to fight for seven more years. In 1980, he fought what would become his penultimate match, against then-champion Larry Holmes. The beating Ali received was so severe Holmes wept after it. Actor Sylvester Stallone described it as 'like watching an autopsy on a man who's still alive'.

After his final loss in 1981, Ali retired. Three years later he was diagnosed with Parkinson's disease. The punches he took over a long career were crucial to his condition. Despite the decline and severity of his condition, Ali simply could not give up.

As Duke writes, 'While grit can get you to stick to hard things that are worthwhile, grit can also get you to stick to hard things that are no longer worthwhile. The trick is figuring out the difference'.

This section covers three stocks where we failed to figure out the difference.

There is a unique unhappiness about buying a company, watching the investment case come apart and then failing to act quickly enough to limit the damage. These are not the most devastating errors – those are reserved for Part II – but they are the most common.

The reason is as Duke describes. Grit is what makes value investing work. The ability to do what others cannot – to find a cheap stock and buy it when everyone else is screaming 'sell' – is central to it.

It can also be the source of error, mainly because the act of purchasing a stock deepens the commitment to it. When that happens, the grit is already in the gears. Reversing when you expected to accelerate is like trying to jam a fish into a sock: most people simply cannot even contemplate it.

Investing is more capricious and less predictable than we imagine, an art as much as a science. Errors are inevitable, with this book proof of it. Not acting fast enough to sell stocks that weren't playing out as we expected is the source of most of our errors. This is where the agonies and sleepless nights lie: the red flags ignored, the clues missed in ASX announcements, the complexities neglected and the pride that got in the way.

The sharemarket excels at crushing the egos of the overconfident and ill-informed. If one is prepared to accept hard truths brutally dispatched, the opportunities to learn are as plentiful as they are painful.

Each of the three following case studies created painful and necessary scars. Growth is not in the success that confirms our brilliance but in the failures that confound and nearly break us. The grit that is required to examine them is as necessary as that required to buy the stocks in the first place.

While the sources of failure were different in each case, they are bound together by a primal question: after making up our minds about a stock and putting money behind it, in the face of changing facts, why didn't we change our minds? This part of the book endeavours to answer that question.

Case study #1
Strathfield Car Radios

Jive in and flail away

When Andrew Kelly was selling car radios in Sydney's bustling Paddy's Markets, he couldn't have expected to one day feature on the *BRW Rich List*, nor imagine the collapse of the business that put him there. Kelly rode the mobile phone revolution, first to success and then to disaster, and we followed his every step down.

What happened

The first *Intelligent Investor* office was in the architectural wasteland of Bondi Junction. The forlorn environment was well represented by a giant red sarcophagus of a building occupied by Strathfield Car Radios. Had the remains of Chairman Mao been secretly buried in Sydney's eastern suburbs, this is where one might have found them.

Strathfield's arrival was prescient. Telstra had released the first 1G phone on its analogue network in 1987, retailing for a staggering $4,250.[1] Strathfield, a retailer and installer of car phones, began selling mobile phones that same year. Kelly had realised sooner than most

---

1   telstrawholesale.com.au/wholesaleconnect/category/technology/mobile-history-part-1.html

that mobiles would be huge and wanted a part of the action. In 1990, just 1 percent of Australians had a mobile phone. Ten years later, that figure had increased to almost 50 percent.[2] Strathfield was riding the wave beautifully.

Recognising that competition would inevitably increase, Kelly carpet-bombed Sydney's airwaves with in-your-face TV and radio advertising. The company's jingle – 'drive in and jive away' – became a part of the cultural vernacular, a symbol of a sales-driven organisation with a voice as loud as the paint on its walls. Today, copycat advertising from Harvey Norman and JB Hi-Fi echoes the Strathfield approach.

It was intrusive and effective. By 1998, Strathfield had 58 stores across the country. About two-thirds of the company's $150 million in annual revenue came from mobile phone sales and commissions. Automotive electronics such as alarms and CD players, once the company's bread and butter, were diminishing in their importance. Through its exclusive relationship with Telstra, Strathfield had become one of the nation's largest mobile retailers.

Flushed with success, Strathfield listed on the Australian Securities Exchange (ASX) in July 1998, issuing 61 million shares at $1.70.[3] Kelly's founding stake had made him wealthy. With more than 50 percent of the company, he had his eyes on greater riches. Covering the country in Strathfield stores was how he was going to do it.

Specialty retailers like Strathfield can be challenging investments. Most struggle with high rents, operate in competitive fields and fight to establish a niche that offers even mediocre returns. Investing in them is a bit like sitting on a cracked toilet – a small shift in the foundations can end in disaster.

The best time to buy is when they're in rollout mode, taking a proven, established concept from, say, a handful of stores to hundreds. In 1998 Strathfield was in rollout mode and charging up the S-curve. The sigmoid curve, as it is formally known, describes how a product

---

2   skwirk.com.au/skwirk/uploadFiles/content/database/files/chapter.1868.body.html
3   2 July 1988, ASX.com.au, Admission to Official List

or market (or virus, for that matter) progresses through the various stages of its lifecycle (see Figure 3). Understanding this and identifying where a company is in its lifecycle is essential to successful investing.

Figure 3: The S-curve

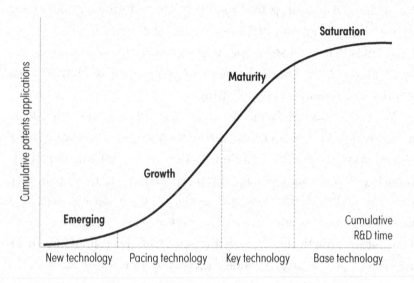

The mobile sector provides a classic example of an S-curve. When Telstra launched its first car phone, few purchased it except 'yuppies', who were disparaged and deemed 'up themselves' for doing so. Marketers call these people 'early adopters'. This is the emerging phase, when the idea is seeded but yet to take off with the general public. With product improvements, price reductions and improved mobile coverage came rapid growth. This phase lasted around a decade, before growth began to plateau as the market became saturated. Mobile phone sales are now in decline; like the pager, telex and fax machine, mobile phones will likely be superseded one day by superior technology.

A similar dynamic is evident in specialty retailers. With clever management, some can extend their S-curve, but most cannot escape it.

Former brands such as Brashs and Dick Smith (both electronics) and Roger David (menswear) have disappeared, and department stores are edging towards obscurity. Everything has a limited lifespan.

At the time of Strathfield's listing, Kelly correctly believed it was near the beginning of its S-curve. There was plenty of growth ahead. A year later, it was deep into rollout mode and growing like Topsy, forecasting sales growth of 12 percent but delivering a figure almost three times that. New store openings were key. Planning to open ten stores in the 1999 financial year, Strathfield opened 31 in just six months. The rollout was in full swing.

What analysts call 'same-store sales', or 'like-for-like sales', were also growing. This is a critical measure. A retailer can easily boost sales simply by opening additional stores, but often this negatively impacts per-store sales. A good specialty retailer will be able to open lots of new stores and enjoy increasing per-store sales growth. The same-store sales metric reveals the performance of existing stores while 'store growth' focuses on the speed of the rollout. From an investment perspective, a retailer increasing same-store sales whilst also opening new stores and having them reach profitability quickly is the perfect combination.

By January 1999, Strathfield's store openings were flying, and same-store sales had increased by an impressive 15 percent. Crucially, most Australians had yet to purchase a mobile phone. Here was a stock perfectly placed on its S-curve. Kelly had proved the model, everything was ahead of it, and it was cheap. At $1.85, with a prospective dividend yield of almost 6 percent and a price earnings ratio (PER) under 12, well below the All Ordinaries' average of over 19 percent, we wanted a piece of the action. No one in the *Intelligent Investor* team had any idea of the disaster it would become.

Things began well enough. In the next financial year, sales rose by over a third, same-store sales increased 11 percent and profitability ballooned. With plans to open another ten stores, Strathfield was in the sweet spot.

Other moves were afoot. Kelly purchased Eworld, a company making software for handheld computers, and engaged in some succession planning. With the dotcom boom in full flight, Kelly nominated himself as the new general manager and chief executive in charge of 'new opportunities'. By February of 2000, Strathfield's share price had risen to around $3.50 and Kelly made his move, raising $15 million to develop ecommerce business ideas through what became known as Strathfield E-Ventures, with Eworld at its foundation. Kelly was all in on the dotcom frenzy.

The so-called TMT sector – technology, media and telecoms – of which Strathfield was a part, was the foundation of the dotcom bubble. When the bubble began to burst, there was no escape. The momentum that had carried Strathfield's share price up to $3.50 began to operate in reverse, and there was little Kelly could do about it.

Just a few months after launching Strathfield E-Ventures, Strathfield announced its profits would be much lower than forecast. Kelly blamed it on Telstra, which was not 'competitive with other networks'.[4] He set about refashioning the business. The Telstra agreement was the first to go, replaced by an open-house model where all three mobile networks were sold in Strathfield stores. An expansion into home electronics, including televisions and DVD players, was also announced. And just four months after it spearheaded Strathfield E-Ventures, Kelly announced that Eworld would be sold.

By mid-2000, the share price was down more than 50 percent from its dotcom highs and more than 25 percent from our original buy recommendation. Kelly and fellow Strathfield board member Carl Olsen were unperturbed. Both were buying shares on the way down. Insider buying, as it is known, is usually a good sign for external shareholders. When those who know the company best are loading up, there are usually good reasons to hang on.

The full-year results announced in August 2000 crushed that belief. Sales growth was negligible and net profit after tax dropped

---

4   intelligentinvestor.com.au/recommendations/strathfield-hits-a-wall/49117

34 percent. Displaying the natural optimism of a company founder, Kelly called the result an 'aberration'.

Many rapidly growing businesses face near-death experiences. This was Strathfield's. The company had grown too quickly, with too many unprofitable stores, and had lost focus on what had made it successful.

A painful but necessary period of cost-cutting began. Of the company's 120 stores, 12 were closed.

The results for the year to June 2001 looked promising. Sales had increased by almost 11 percent and same-store sales rose over 6 percent. With the share price languishing at $1, we backed the turnaround and Kelly's self-interest in continuing to lead it.

The dawn proved to be false. In its early days, Strathfield had become synonymous with mobile phones. Its stores were where consumers went to get one. Growing competition and an ever-expanding product range undermined that proposition. Strathfield had lost its brand leadership and, with it, a path to reinvention. Cash flow, the lifeblood of every business, was becoming a problem. In 2001, Strathfield recorded more than $12 million in operating cash flow. Two years later, that figure had dropped to an outflow of $14 million. In the 2004 financial year, it bled another $10 million.

With Strathfield on the edge of bankruptcy, the banks weren't interested in providing a lifeline. Shareholders had to step up or see their stakes disappear. The company issued convertible notes and conducted two rights issues at share prices more than 90 percent below the original listing price. In sheer desperation, it also borrowed from a privately owned finance group.

The impact was catastrophic. At the end of June 2002, Strathfield had 72 million shares on issue and was trading at a price of 31 cents. By July 2004, it had almost 300 million shares on issue. The pie had become smaller and almost four times as many mouths were eating at it. The dilution had pushed the share price down to 12 cents. Strathfield was on life support.

We were as eager for a turnaround as the directors buying shares in the company, but on 8 August 2003, we finally bit the bullet, issuing a clear sell recommendation at 14 cents.

The company struggled on but never recovered. When the board eventually called in the administrators in 2009, with the company still operating more than 75 outlets but owing $37 million[5], its shares were trading below a single cent.

Our investment in Strathfield had begun with huge promise and ended in a loss of 93 percent. It was our first big disaster.

Why it happened

Analysing the reasons for a catastrophic investment loss is like watching a 24-hour episode of *Air Crash Investigations*. With the benefit of time, one can see how a series of compounding errors can turn a tricky situation into a fully-fledged disaster.

Over time, the aviation industry has improved its safety record. Redundancy, an engineering concept whereby backup systems take over when a key component or process fails, has helped. So too have cockpit checklists that reduce human error and technological advances, such as the traffic collision avoidance system (TCAS) and radar.

Professional fund managers have adopted the aviation industry's approach but with far less success. A chat with a fund manager will yield multiple mentions of their 'process', the secret sauce that helps them pick big winners and escape disaster. To impress rating agencies and reassure clients, fund managers produce pithy 80-slide presentations and lengthy documents.

Unfortunately, investing is not like flying a plane. It is entirely rational for a young pilot embarking on their career to believe they will finish it without crashing. The opposite is true in investing.

---

5   smartcompany.com.au/finance/economy/retail-chain-strathfield-collapses-into-administration/

Crashes are guaranteed. The best we can hope for is to learn from them and reduce their incidence. As the aphorism goes, 'Good judgment comes from experience, and experience comes from bad judgment'.

Around the time of our first Strathfield buy recommendation, we needed more experience. Reading the appropriate investing books and Buffett's shareholder letters, and running our own portfolios for years (as most of us had), was only the start. Losing money, feeling foolish and doubting yourself is the price of getting better. Analysing your mistakes is the work.

Here are the red flags that should have made us act sooner.

1. A shaky business model

Strathfield once solved a genuine customer need. Customers could 'drive in and jive away' by combining a car radio purchase with installation. It was a unique pitch that required technical expertise. In comparison, selling mobiles was a cinch. The mobile networks advertised to get customers to Strathfield's stores. Once inside, staff helped them choose a model, do the paperwork and connect to a network. Unlike car radios, almost anyone could sell a mobile phone and get it connected to a network. Within a few years, almost anyone did.

Strathfield's advantage was its large store network, but it operated in a sector where barriers to entry were coming down. Strathfield's moat, as competitive advantage is sometimes known, was shrinking rather than widening. The company was also exposed to economic slowdowns and, eventually, online sales that didn't require a store visit at all. Its 'lock' on customers was loosening. For a few years, Strathfield's numbers gave it the appearance of a high-quality, growing business. Underneath, it was seriously flawed.

2. A store rollout problem

Retail stores are expensive to fit out, stock and staff. Thanks to leasing contracts, closing them is also costly. In any rollout, choosing suitable locations and quickly closing ailing stores is critical. Strathfield got this wrong, further exposing its business model weaknesses. The company expanded quickly, incautiously and, eventually, unprofitably. When the crash came and sales started to fall, inability to cut costs and close stores to keep pace with declining sales exposed the business to the looming cash flow crisis that was its downfall.

3. The gold rush effect

Every bubble is built on genuine promise. It is the excitement around it that does the damage. In 1998, it was a good bet that one day everyone would own a mobile phone. The excitement over this rapidly growing market was obvious. Its impact on supply was less so.

In any gold rush effect, expected future demand inevitably increases supply. To their cost, investors tend to focus on the demand side of the equation and neglect the effects on supply. With mobile phone retailers springing up like weeds, industry competition increased and margins declined. Strathfield stores that were once profitable quickly became loss makers, not because the company overestimated demand but because it underestimated the impact of that demand on inducing supply.

4. Key supplier risk

If bought at sensible prices, Bunnings, Coles and Woolworths can be excellent investments, because their capacity to monopolise demand delivers market power. If a farmer wants to sell thousands of pumpkins, she can't avoid a supermarket chain. The same goes for Bunnings and its cheap garden hoses and hammocks. Being a gatekeeper to customers allows these chains to play off suppliers against each other, capturing margins that wouldn't otherwise be possible.

Strathfield had only one supplier – Telstra – and that left it dauntingly exposed. Kelly whinging about its lack of competitiveness highlighted the problem: if Telstra faltered, so did Strathfield. It was also dependent on Telstra for its advertising campaigns to drive customers into stores, and on credits and subsidies to support their purchases. Telstra, which cared only for overall mobile connections, effectively controlled Strathfield's destiny.

5. Lack of focus

Famed 1980s fund manager Peter Lynch invented the term 'diworsification' to describe an acquisition or an extension into a new area that reduces the quality of the company undertaking it. Kelly had enjoyed a good run, jumping first on drivers' desire to have better sound in their cars and then climbing aboard the mobile phone revolution. His next moves were both examples of diworsification.

Expanding into home office products, acquiring Eworld and launching Strathfield E-Ventures to take advantage of the dotcom hype indicated an overconfident management team needing more focus. By the time they returned to what initially made the business successful, it was too late.

Lessons

Strathfield Car Radios, our first huge error, was a result of some elemental investing mistakes. Here are the lessons we learned from it.

1. Seeing is one thing, acting is another

What's remarkable about the multitude of red flags Strathfield displayed was not that we missed them but that we spelled out each one in our first detailed analysis of the company in January 1999. We had recognised where this stock might go wrong from the first moment we looked at it.

However, when presented with the evidence that confirmed the risks we had identified, we steadfastly ignored it. Instead, we pursued Kelly and co. all the way down. Confirmation bias – the tendency to interpret information that supports prior beliefs – explains why. Having recommended Strathfield, believing it to be undervalued and likely to deliver attractive future returns, we became less likely to acknowledge information contradicting that view. We fell victim to confirmation bias.

2. Following the smart money isn't always smart

A small, high-growth company is more likely to be a good investment if it is led by a founder with a sizable stake in the business. In the lingua franca of value investing, this is known as 'following the smart money' or 'eating your own cooking'. Before all the rights issues, Kelly owned a massive 56 percent of Strathfield. He wasn't just eating his own cooking; he was gorging on it and, via subsequent director transactions, going back for seconds every time the share price fell.

Unfortunately, the smart money can also be dumb for the same reasons we were. Kelly, determined to make a go of the business he had spent two decades building, was just as guilty of confirmation bias as we were. His misplaced confidence, expressed through his insider purchases, encouraged our own.

3. Overcoming confirmation bias is crucial

There is no shortcut to overcoming this psychological banana skin, but there are techniques to reduce its impact. Awareness is the first step. If you've spent decades building a business, or concluded after months analysing it that it is worthy of investment, you have been primed to view new information favourably. Being aware of this helps.

Second, having developed a view on a stock, actively look for information that challenges it. If you've made an argument to buy a stock, make the case for selling it, too. This will help you acknowledge information you may not want to see. If you find this difficult, seek out someone who has come to the opposite conclusion. Be willing to change your mind in the face of new evidence.

Two practical steps may help you develop this mindset. The first is to write a short note for each stock you purchase that formalises how you expect the business to develop over the next three to five years – a roadmap of sorts. This might include rough sales forecasts, profitability expectations, investment in research and development, and expansion plans. Laying out your expectations for a business will make it easier to see when it starts to veer off track. Had we done this with Strathfield, I doubt we would have held it for so long and lost so much.

The second step is more radical. The act of buying a stock makes us more committed to it. The act of holding it, perhaps for years, exacerbates this tendency. Both acts make recognising when a company is going off the rails more difficult. As new information comes to light, confirmation bias interprets it more favourably.

When confronted with new information that might imply the investment case has weakened, some investors immediately sell a stock. The purpose is to evaluate the new information free from confirmation bias. Selling makes that easier. If, after examining all the new evidence, you decide you want to remain invested, you can buy back in.

This may have tax implications and will increase trading costs; it may also mean missing out if the stock suddenly recovers, though of course this can work both ways. But some investors feel it is the best way to be free of the mental shackles of ownership. These tactics will help you make fewer mistakes, although they won't eliminate them entirely.

Aftermath

If you ache for a hard, demanding life, open a specialty retailer and watch your dreams come true. Take pleasure from the endless, brutal competition, thin margins and astronomical rents. And if you make even average returns, give yourself a pat on the back. In this business, you must be dedicated and talented just to stay alive.

Whilst riches await those who crack the formula of a unique retail concept, few wear the crown. Strathfield was one of a string of business failures in mobile phone retailing. The major carriers now have their own store networks, and so-called mobile virtual network operators (MVNOs) such as Kogan Mobile, Amaysim (see Case Study #9) and Lebara piggyback on them with sharply priced retail offers. Tough, competitive markets consolidate, with the spoils going to the most powerful players in the value chain – in this case Telstra and Optus, and of course the phone manufacturers such as Apple and Samsung.

In specialty fashion retailing, recent chain closures include Jeanswest, Seafolly, G-Star RAW and ESPRIT. Over the past few decades, only JB Hi-Fi (a truly exceptional business), Flight Centre and, more recently, Lovisa, currently rolling out internationally, have endured and prospered. Still, qualifications are needed. JB Hi-Fi has only expanded into New Zealand (and should be credited for not trying to go further). Flight Centre still operates in South Africa, Canada and the UK but has expanded into corporate travel as its leisure business struggles with the shift to online bookings. And Lovisa remains a long way from reaching its true potential. With its focus on selling disposable jewellery to faddish young adults, there remains a chance it may not.

With a small population, high rents and blistering competition, Australia has been a specialty retailing graveyard. Andrew Kelly eventually got the message. As the share price of Strathfield fell, so did his fortune.

But don't feel too sorry for him. In 2000, Kelly purchased a block of land from the Sydney Harbour Foreshore Authority for $52 million and established a joint venture with Multiplex to develop it.[6] His timing was again perfect. Three years later, Kelly sold down his majority interest, reputedly for $216 million.[7] In 2005, he retired from Strathfield and moved to Hong Kong.[8]

Strathfield Car Radios now operates from a single store in, yes, Strathfield in western Sydney – the location of his first outlet.

---

6   afr.com/property/52m-buy-generates-static-20010419-k0xdl
7   afr.com/property/kelly-switches-off-216m-harbour-play-20030314-k20gl
8   applianceretailer.com.au/vahjbbgiif/

After non-payment of annual listing fees, the company was delisted from the ASX in August 2013.[9]

No doubt Kelly enjoyed the ride and came out ahead, but we learnt our lesson, steering clear of most speciality retailers until Lovisa joined the buy list at a price of $11.10 in early 2020. Things have gone well since, but with the Strathfield experience etched into our memory, we'll be the first to get out if the investment case ever veers off course.

REFERENCES

- 29 Jan 1999: Strathfield wired for growth (intelligentinvestor.com.au/recommendations/strathfield-wired-for-growth/47678)
- 26 Feb 1999: Strathfield sets the pace (intelligentinvestor.com.au/recommendations/strathfield-sets-the-pace/47751)
- 10 Sep 1999: Strathfield rings up a great result and a great future (intelligentinvestor.com.au/recommendations/strathfield-rings-up-a-great-result-and-a-great-future/48290)
- 11 Feb 2000: Strathfield's little dot.com adventure (intelligentinvestor.com.au/investment-news/strathfields-little-dotcom-adventure/48735)
- 2 Jun 2000: Strathfield hits a wall (intelligentinvestor.com.au/recommendations/strathfield-hits-a-wall/49117)
- 10 Aug 2001: Is Strathfield still jiving? (intelligentinvestor.com.au/recommendations/is-strathfield-still-jiving/50400)
- 8 Aug 2003: Strathfield Group (intelligentinvestor.com.au/recommendations/strathfield-group-limited/52817)
- 16 Sep 2004: Sizing up Strathfield (intelligentinvestor.com.au/investment-news/sizing-up-strathfield/53939)

---

9   delisted.com.au/company/strathfield-group-limited/

Case Study #2
Roc Oil

When love and loss collide

When a genial Welshman who had made a fortune at his previous company walked into our office, it was love at first sight. Despite an acquisition we were convinced would turn bad, the impression he left was so great that even after he died, we couldn't let go.

What happened

Geologists comprehend the true meaning of time in a way most of us do not. Rocks can do that to a person. Those working in the capricious world of resource exploration exemplify the breed. With disappointment and loss drilled into them, they are the undertakers of the investment world. Unlike many of their projects, they tend not to get carried away.

Former geologist and Roc Oil chief executive John Doran was modest, thoughtful and brimming with Welsh charm. Sometimes, well before it became fashionable, he wore t-shirts under his suit jacket. I didn't know what it meant to fall in love with a stock until I met him. With the benefit of hindsight, I was primed to do so. Doran reminded me of my Welsh grandfather, thoughtlessly buried by my own father at exactly the time the 1974 World Cup final kicked off. I have never quite forgiven him for that, but despite a 60 percent loss on Roc Oil, I have excused John Doran.

A respected oil man, Doran's previous position was chief executive at Command Petroleum, formerly Cluff Oil. He took the position in 1992 and sold the company a few years later to Scottish group Cairn Energy, delivering an almost fivefold increase to shareholders, which included himself. Roc Oil was Doran's next play.

Many view investing as a horse race, and for those buying stocks on the word of a friend or family member, it is. Resource exploration stocks – companies looking for oil, gold, coal and the like – are doubly so. The attraction of Roc was its portfolio of exciting possibilities, combined with assets already producing at impressive margins. If none of the speculative plays came off, the collapse would not be total. Roc Oil was a punt with plenty of potential and a comfy backstop.

The company had oil and gas exploration activities in Australia but also operated in Equatorial Guinea, Angola, Mauritania and China. In investing, this is called sovereign, or country, risk. In Africa especially, it is common for a government to claim ownership of a mine, or extract what might be called 'informal royalties' that end up in a Swiss bank account.

Roc's exposure was minimised through assets acquired at reasonable prices, with no single project dominating. If one or two failed, shareholders might suffer a few rips, but they would keep their shirts. Roc wasn't going to zero.

The backstop was provided by exploration projects already producing healthy cash flows, including Cliff Head off the Western Australian coast and gas-producing assets at Saltfleetby and Keddington in the United Kingdom. At 75 percent, the operating cash flow margin was spectacular. Since production started in 1999, net reserves had increased, because Roc was finding more gas faster than it could sell it. By our reckoning, these assets alone were worth over $100 million. Roc also had a net cash position of around $45 million.

A toddler could have done the sums. If the African and Chinese exploration projects came to naught, the stock was still worth at least $145 million. With 108 million shares on issue at a price of $1.13, Roc Oil had a market capitalisation of $122 million. We were paying for the production assets but getting the speculative exploration portfolio for free. This was a resources stock with a margin of safety.

Management was an added attraction. Doran had been one of the first to explore for oil in India, and many in the management team had African experience. They were also heavily invested in their own performance: Doran owned 4 percent of Roc's stock and senior management collectively owned 15 percent. If Roc was going down, management was going with it. That was just how we liked it.

In June 2003, at a price of $1.13, Roc Oil joined our buy list. It would be almost seven years before we recommended selling. By then, Doran had tragically died, and members had lost a lot of money.

Things got off to a flyer. By July 2006, Roc's share price had risen above $4. It had also acquired, at an attractive price, a stake in a block in the South China Sea where initial tests were encouraging. At Cabinda in Angola, seismic data was also promising. This was a world-class oil region where billions of barrels of oil had already been discovered.

We doubled down on our initial recommendation at what turned out to be the top. At the time of our ignominious exit in 2010, the share price had fallen to 45 cents.

Making mistakes in small resource stocks is inevitable. Either there is enough of the resource in the ground to warrant getting it out or there isn't. That wasn't the case with Roc. What destroyed it was a classic error we couldn't imagine this competent, dedicated management team making.

Mergers and acquisitions – M&A in the lingo – are the banana skins of the investing world. *Harvard Business Review* suggests that more than two in every three fails.[1] Much like a newly wedded couple

---

1   hbr.org/2020/03/dont-make-this-common-ma-mistake

denying the possibility of divorce, an acquisitive chief executive and board will insist that the law of averages won't apply to them. This is the Lake Wobegon effect[2], a tendency for humans to overestimate their own abilities. Lake Wobegon, a fictional town created by Garrison Keillor as a part of his US radio program, is a place where 'all the women are strong, all the men are good-looking, and all the children are above average'. It is also where every M&A deal works out perfectly.

We knew this in June 2008 when Roc Oil announced plans to acquire Anzon Australia and its 52 percent shareholder, UK-listed Anzon Energy. This was an all-scrip deal: shares would be exchanged between the two companies in lieu of cash. No money was involved. Instead, Roc would double its number of shares on issue in exchange for Anzon's assets, most of which were in the Basker Manta Gummy (BMG) development in the Bass Strait, deemed to be worth about $500 million.

The deal was sold on the basis that it would more than double Roc's net reserves to 47 million barrels of oil equivalent and deliver more predictable cash flows, especially from politically 'safe' countries. We weren't persuaded, the analyst writing in June 2008:

> Nothing in the information released so far makes me think Roc's odds of success are substantially different from the general experience. We're giving away too much potential upside in exchange for a little downside protection. And that downside protection won't even cover us against some of the bigger risks, like a lower oil price.

That article featured a misleading company chart showing a rapid increase in the expected daily production profile of the newly merged entity. What it failed to show was the reduced share of the merged entity's production accruing to Roc's existing shareholders. We re-ran the numbers to account for current shareholders' smaller share of the

---

2   en.wikipedia.org/wiki/Lake_Wobegon

merged company and found production per share would *reduce* in 2008, 2009 and 2010.

The article pleaded with management to abandon the deal because of what shareholders were relinquishing to make it happen. Roc's share price significantly undervalued the company's assets and prospects, a position John Doran had publicly conceded. Using it as a currency to acquire an asset that shouldn't have been on the agenda, using charts that misrepresented reality, was hard to fathom.

We wondered how Doran agreed to such a deal, suspecting the board was forcing it through. Knowing thousands of members owned Roc stock on our say-so, the company requested a meeting. Doran wanted to talk us through the deal. It would be one of the last meetings he would hold.

Doran was charming and persuasive. After expressing our concerns, he reassured us that he supported the deal and wasn't being strong-armed by the board. After he left, an attendee remarked that he didn't look well. A few days later, the company announced that John Doran had died after a short illness.

The $500 million Anzon acquisition was a lemon, as we suspected. Within a few years, proven and probable reserves were downgraded by about 80 percent. Roc shareholders had paid over the odds for a dud, and the company's technical team had dramatically overestimated the value of Anzon's primary asset.

The deal was like the goldfish that floats to the top of the tank, like finding that Lake Wobegon is full of dead fish. It was the final straw. We sold out at a price of 45 cents in February 2010. From beginning to end, the loss was 60 percent. For those who bought following our recommendations in 2006, at above $4, that figure was closer to 90 percent.

Why it happened

The error had four basic sources.

1. Our recommendation was misleading

Losing money in speculative situations is to be expected. If you allocate only a small part of your portfolio to them, the damage will be contained. Roc was not a high-quality company like CSL or Woolworths, but its high-margin, cash-generating operations in the UK offered a backstop to potential losses. Exemplary returns depended on finding oil in high-risk countries. Any company on which the investment case depends on a slice of luck, a discovery or the commercialisation of a new idea or process is speculative. We did not call Roc a speculative investment when it clearly was.

2. We fell in love with a CEO

Doran's experience, credentials and personability made us susceptible to narrative bias. Because he'd made money for shareholders previously, we were willing to believe he'd do so again. As new facts emerged, we interpreted them to support this narrative, downplaying the capricious nature of oil exploration.

3. Commitment bias took over

Once narrative bias took hold, the danger of commitment bias – the tendency to stick to previously expressed opinions or views – increased. There are parallels with Strathfield Car Radios, but Roc was different. Between June 2003 and March 2009, we made 44 buy recommendations on Roc, an average of more than seven a year. Each added to our commitment. That made it harder to change our view when the facts changed.

4. We saw a giant red flag and ignored it

Despite these faults, we may still have made money on Roc were it not for one fateful decision.

The Anzon acquisition turned $500 million into a dollar. Our scathing review of it at the time got everything right except the recommendation: instead of selling, we downgraded to 'hold'. This was the fateful error. A charismatic CEO, and narrative and commitment bias, combined to cause it.

Lessons

Here are the lessons we learned from investing in Roc Oil.

1. When the facts change, re-examine your view

It is possible to make the right decision and get the wrong result. Putting Roc on the buy list was not an error. The stock was cheap, and the potential was clear. Our error was in not adjusting to the new facts as they emerged.

2. Apply a portfolio limit

Prior to Roc Oil, members determined how much of their portfolio they allocated to an individual stock. Many were overexposed to Roc as a result. After it, we introduced maximum recommended portfolio weightings to provide better guidance. On speculative stocks, the maximum weighting is typically limited to between 2 and 3 percent. Sensible portfolio weightings are a useful way of managing the risk of speculative investments not working out.

3. Beware the charismatic CEO

Egotistical CEOs are easy to spot. They tend to use 'I' rather than 'we', they relentlessly plug their business to get the share price (and the value of their options) up, they interrupt board members and senior management in public meetings, and they rarely admit a mistake. They make it all about them. In small, speculative stocks, they are best avoided.

Founder CEOs like John Doran and Strathfield's Andrew Kelly are more difficult to assess because they are more believable and likeable. Both were also heavily invested in the businesses they were running. Backing such people often pays off because their incentives are aligned with shareholders, but these personal factors can obscure more pertinent business metrics. If you love a CEO, that can be just as big a warning sign as despising one.

4. There's no substitute for expertise and research

Investing cannot be done on a whim. Figuring out if a stock is undervalued requires more than a feeling and a three-point checklist. No amount of screening can replace a deep dive into a company's business and financial fundamentals. If you're not prepared to do that, or lack access to people who are, expect more than your fair share of painful mistakes.

Aftermath

Roc Oil wasn't the biggest loss in our history, but it might have been the most valuable, provoking changes in how we researched companies and made decisions. It was a failure that strengthened rather than broke us.

In addition to introducing portfolio limits on each stock we recommended, we started a *Dragons' Den* process for buy recommendations that continues to this day. Whilst each analyst covers a stock, the team has input into the recommendation and an opportunity to put forward opposing views. Recommendation changes also require group input.

This is useful because proximity can be a problem. Outsiders can sometimes see the bigger picture more clearly *because* they know less about the company. If you're managing your own money, a small group of like-minded souls with a similar investment approach is a useful way to increase the diversity of opinion and minimise errors.

We also developed a management checklist to mitigate the risk of falling in love with a CEO. Some are better than others, but underlying business dynamics and industry structure tend to have a greater bearing on investment success. A good CEO helps but is far from the only factor. If you pit an exceptional CEO against a poor business, it is usually the poor business that wins out. High-quality businesses are more important to investing success than capable, personable CEOs. Having both is ideal.

REFERENCES

- 25 Jun 2003: Roc's on a roll (intelligentinvestor.com.au/recommendations/rocs-on-a-roll/52681)
- 19 Feb 2004: Price and value rising at Roc Oil (intelligentinvestor.com.au/recommendations/price-and-value-rising-at-roc-oil/53343)
- 2 Sep 2004: Breaking Roc down (intelligentinvestor.com.au/recommendations/breaking-roc-down/53907)
- 24 May 2006: Roc strikes oil in South China Sea (intelligentinvestor.com.au/recommendations/roc-strikes-oil-in-south-china-sea/55057)
- 13 Sep 2006: Running the rule over Roc Oil (intelligentinvestor.com.au/recommendations/running-the-rule-over-roc/55285)
- 7 Nov 2006: Roc Oil passes around the cap (intelligentinvestor.com.au/recommendations/roc-oil-passes-around-the-cap/55432)
- 18 Dec 2006: Roc Oil directors show support (intelligentinvestor.com.au/investment-news/roc-oil-directors-show-support/55552)
- 1 Nov 2007: Much ado about nothing at Roc Oil (intelligentinvestor.com.au/recommendations/much-ado-about-nothing-at-roc-oil/56097)
- 25 Jun 2008: Don't spoil our Roc Oil (intelligentinvestor.com.au/recommendations/dont-spoil-our-roc-oil/56468)
- 13 Jan 2010: Between Roc Oil and a hard place (intelligentinvestor.com.au/recommendations/between-roc-oil-and-a-hard-place/57312)
- 4 Feb 2010: Time to sell Roc Oil? (intelligentinvestor.com.au/recommendations/time-to-sell-roc-oil/57348)

Case Study #3
Star Entertainment

One star, many sinners

Casinos are a licence to print money – or should be. Star Entertainment, which became synonymous with staggering mismanagement, arrogance and ineptitude, proved otherwise. The eventual loss was a hefty 80 percent, the lessons equally weighty.

What happened

Walter Summerford was first struck by lightning while serving as a British officer in World War I.[1] After emigrating to Canada, he took up fishing. In 1924, holding his rod beneath a tree, he endured a second strike.

Six years later, he had recovered enough movement to enjoy a walk in the local park, where he suffered a third strike that left him paralysed. Summerford spent the rest of his days tortured by the belief he was cursed. Perhaps he was. Four years after his death, his gravestone was shattered by a lightning bolt.

The difference between Summerford and Star Entertainment – operator of casinos in Sydney, Brisbane, Perth and the Gold Coast – is

---

1   burialsandbeyond.com/2022/10/29/walter-summerford-the-unluckiest-man-in-the-world/

that Walter Summerford experienced extraordinarily bad luck, whereas the damage sustained by Star was largely self-inflicted.

Casinos can make excellent investments. Like tobacco, opioids and coffee, they sell an addictive, profitable product to people economists would describe as lacking price sensitivity. Addicts and so-called whales – rich gamblers who can drop a cool $10 million on a big night out – are good examples, as are organised crime figures seeking to cover their tracks by money laundering.

Unsurprisingly, casinos are heavily regulated. Compliance is encouraged by the threat of large fines or loss of the licence to operate. There are, however, opposing pressures. State governments have come to rely on gambling taxes, and casinos employ large workforces. The tension is best expressed in the long-term approach to the sector. Whilst regulators and politicians have big sticks at their disposal, they have preferred a light touch.

Our investment case for Star had at its base the belief that this would not change. For decades, light-touch regulation had been a reliable assumption, aptly demonstrated during the pandemic. In July 2020, barely three months after the introduction of social distancing requirements and restrictions on movement and gatherings, the New South Wales Government permitted The Star Sydney casino to reopen. When just 20 people were allowed to attend a wedding, The Star Sydney was permitted up to 5,000 people in its casino.[2]

Within a few months, gaming revenue at The Star Sydney had recovered to 80 percent of the previous corresponding period. In March 2020, we had called Star a buy at a price of $2.20. By June it had risen more than 50 percent. Then the weather changed.

In truth, the first lightning strike hit in 2018[3], but only a few parties were privy to it. KPMG had produced a damning report claiming Star's Sydney casino's anti-money-laundering team was under-resourced,

2 gamblinginsider.com/news/10941/the-star-sydney-to-increase-capacity-to-5000-amid-eased-restrictions
3 abc.net.au/news/2022-03-22/star-casino-inquiry-hears-ceo-sulked-money-laundering-report/100929368#

deeming the risk of money laundering and terrorism financing as high. AUSTRAC, the financial crimes watchdog, requested a copy. Star, claiming legal privilege, denied it.

In Victoria, the Bergin Inquiry report into competitor Crown Casino was released in February 2021, followed by a Royal Commission later that year. Both made findings that echoed KPMG's report on The Star Sydney. The Commission further found that Crown's conduct had been 'illegal, dishonest, unethical and exploitative' and that it was unfit to hold a casino licence.[4] Subsequent casino investigations would be launched across the country.

In January 2022, AUSTRAC expanded an investigation into all Star entities 'for alleged serious and systemic non-compliance with Australia's anti-money laundering and counter-terrorism financing laws'. In March, Star chief executive Matt Bekier resigned after it was claimed he did nothing about the failings itemised in KPMG's report[5], preferring instead to berate the authors.

Later that year, the NSW Independent Casino Commission's Chief Commissioner, Philip Crawford, released his report into Star.[6] The company had painted itself as a cleanskin, even making an audacious $6.6 billion bid for Crown in May 2021. Crawford's report quashed that perception, accusing the company of being 'rotten to the core' and of 'breathtaking institutional arrogance'. Issuing the maximum $100 million fine, Crawford also said that Star was unfit to hold a casino licence. The second bolt had struck. We reworked our numbers.

There was still a question mark over the extent of AUSTRAC's fines, which could be far higher than $100 million. The saviour was Star's Queen's Wharf Brisbane project, which was due to open in 2023.[7] Entering the second half of 2022, Star's debt pile of just over $1 billion looked manageable, with capital expenditure on Queen's

4   abc.net.au/news/2022-10-22/casinos-gambling-industry-get-off-lightly-for-major-law-breaches/101560934
5   abc.net.au/news/2022-03-28/star-casino-ceo-matt-bekier-resigns-inquiry/100943910
6   bbc.co.uk/news/world-australia-63280853
7   en.wikipedia.org/wiki/Queen%27s_Wharf,_Brisbane

Wharf winding down and free cash flow set to rapidly recover. With a remediation plan in place and a special manager to supervise the necessary changes, Star's share price was back at attractive levels. Unaware that the next lightning strike loomed, we switched from 'hold' to 'buy'.

The state casino inquiries had embarrassed governments. For the first time in decades, they had an incentive to act. The Victoria State Government implemented load-up limits on pokie machines and mandatory closures.[8] It also increased taxes on wagering and betting by 50 percent. The NSW Government went further, proposing a top tax rate of 61 percent on pokie machines.[9] After decades of being weak on casinos, casinos were red meat for politicians and regulators wanting to look strong.

The proposed NSW taxes, forecast to raise $364 million over three years, would blow a 20 percent hole in Star's operating profits, enough for the company to breach the covenants with its lenders. To avoid disaster, the company had to act.

In February 2023, Star announced it would raise $800 million to reduce its net debt to around $340 million.[10] Those shareholders who didn't participate experienced an immediate 42 percent fall in the intrinsic value of their holding. In November 2022, Star's share price hovered around $3. After the capital raising it traded at about half that. The collapse had begun.

In April 2023, Star revealed it was experiencing 'a rapid deterioration in operating conditions'.[11] Across Darling Harbour, Crown Sydney had been open for six months. Competition was biting and Star's financial condition was deteriorating. The new NSW Labor Government had reduced the former Liberal Government's proposed tax increases, but in July the tax increases would come into effect.

8   engage.vic.gov.au/landmark-gambling-reforms
9   abc.net.au/news/2023-08-11/nsw-government-overhauls-star-casino-tax-changes-saves-jobs/102717236
10 afr.com/companies/games-and-wagering/star-entertainment-group-enters-trading-halt-mulls-capital-raise-20230222-p5cmj3
11 igamingbusiness.com/finance/star-to-restructure-as-business-warns-of-deteriorating-conditions/

Operating restrictions were also in place under the oversight of regulator-appointed special managers, and there was the prospect of another gaming tax and fine in Queensland. The ongoing AUSTRAC investigation was of even greater concern. In 2020, Westpac had been hit with a $1.3 billion penalty for breaching anti-money-laundering rules.[12] Were Star's fine to be even a third of that, the impact would be catastrophic. The company was now in the hands of state governments, AUSTRAC and, with net debt of almost $600 million, potentially the banks.

In September 2023, another lightning strike turned disaster into farce. The opening of Queen's Wharf Brisbane was delayed to April 2024 and a dispute with the contractor was headed for court. The previous February, management had claimed the $800 million capital raising 'provided increased financial flexibility to navigate a range of operating uncertainties'. Evidently, it wasn't enough. Just seven months after the first capital raising, Star was passing around the hat for another $750 million.[13]

Our analyst wrote at the time, 'We have as much faith in [CEO] Robbie Cooke's "strategic priorities" as homoeopathic wine and dolphin healing'. But the assets were cheap, and a recovery loomed. We hung on.

Then, in late February 2024, the NSW Independent Casino Commission launched another inquiry into the company's unresolved cultural issues and its fitness to hold a casino licence.[14] Star's remediation efforts were deemed inadequate, and what was once unthinkable – the permanent loss of its licence – seemed possible, perhaps even likely.

The possibility of a Summerford-style gravestone lightning strike was the last straw. Having lost faith in the NSW Government's ability to act predictably and Star's capacity to address its own obvious cultural problems, we finally sold out later that month (see Figure 4).

---

12 austrac.gov.au/news-and-media/our-recent-work/westpac-penalty-ordered

13 afr.com/street-talk/star-entertainment-launches-750m-equity-raise-at-60c-a-share-20230925-p5e791

14 nicc.nsw.gov.au/casino-regulation/2024-independent-inquiry-into-star

Since the original buy recommendation in March 2020, the loss was a hefty 80 percent.

Figure 4: Star Entertainment's share price since 21 October 2019

AUD ($)

16 Mar 20: first buy @ $2.20

8 Jun 22: second buy @ $2.86

20 Feb 24: sell @ $0.43

Jan 20   Jul 20   Jan 21   Jul 21   Jan 22   Jul 22   Jan 23   Jul 23   Jan 24

Why it happened

Star, said our analyst reflecting on the ever-expanding disaster, had 'expanded Murphy's law into a complete legal system: regulatory tightening, tax increases, class actions, the loss of its Sydney monopoly, Queen's Wharf delays, creditor issues, an AUSTRAC investigation, and the pandemic. It's a miracle Star Sydney hasn't been hit by an asteroid'.

An asteroid strike may have been preferable, quickly releasing the land value without the costs of demolition. The loss of one of Australia's ugliest buildings would have been a bonus. As for shareholders, if they must face the death of a company, best that it be quick.

There were three elemental reasons why our Star recommendation went bad.

1. Governments finally did something

Casinos had been running their own show for decades. Shamed into action by investigative journalists such as Nick McKenzie and the independent state reports, governments were eventually forced to act.

At the time of our initial buy recommendation, we considered this a low-probability risk. The extent of the breaches and the criminal nature of the transgressions revealed in the reports increased that probability.

After being weak for decades, governments and regulators, formerly viewed as invertebrates by the casinos, found a backbone. The fines, higher taxes, special managers and threat of licence loss restricted operating conditions. Collectively, this changed Star's cost base and earnings potential, undoing the investment case as the imposed measures escalated.

2. Debt increased risk

Whilst we initially thought Star's debt was manageable, certain events, including rising interest rates, conspired to make it less so. Just about everything that could go wrong did go wrong. Star may not have entered bankruptcy, at least not at the time of writing, but excessive debt increased the probability of it.

3. Management was inept, and the culture was rotten

Former Star chief executive Matt Bekier berated the authors of KPMG's report for uncovering the behaviours that subsequently crushed the company. This was an example of the company's broader culture, as were the events leading to the resignation of chairman David Foster.[15]

In the company's dealings with regulators and its conduct during the two capital raisings, both of which were non-renounceable, incompetence and lack of trust was evident. To assert that Star was sufficiently funded and then announce an $800 million capital raising was alarming. To conduct another capital raising a mere seven months later, this time for $750 million, was unforgivable.

Denial, obfuscation and prevarication were part of Star's standard operating procedure. Bekier's response to the KPMG report revealed

---

15 reuters.com/business/star-entertainment-executive-chair-foster-steps-down-adds-management-exodus-2024-04-28/

an arrogant culture that deflected criticism and blame, a culture that persisted even after a special manager had been installed. Foster's acts confirmed them, not that this was needed. A deeply rotten ethos had permeated every level of Star, and the removal of a few key personnel was unlikely to change it.

Lessons

Here are the lessons we learned from investing in Star Entertainment.

1. Low-probability events happen

There is a world where an 80 percent loss is not a mistake. Every company faces a million different futures. Wars break out, aeroplanes crash, and governments change taxes and implement new ones. And some chief executives are honest and capable while others are mediocre or crooked. The world is too complex to reliably assess the probability of every factor that may affect the future value of a business. You should, however, assess the most significant risks and assign a probability to them.

Star was hit by multiple lightning bolts. From Royal Commissions to special managers, tax increases, pandemics and construction cost blowouts, everything that could go wrong did. These were low-probability events, but that does not deny their possibility. Occasionally, as Walter Summerford learned, everything that can go wrong does.

The world is less knowable than we like to believe. Only in retrospect do inherently probabilistic situations like our decision to recommend Star seem right or wrong. It is possible to make the right decision and get the wrong result. Our mistake was not buying Star in the first place but failing to get out when management conducted its second capital raising. Arguably, the KPMG report should have provoked an exit, too. We all need some humility in the face of error (and success), because unlikely events happen, and we will lose money when they do.

2. Governments eventually do things

In the same way councils provide a zebra crossing after a kid gets hit by a car, casinos will only be properly regulated once the public realises the gaming floor is stacked with money launderers. These risks might not materialise for decades, but if they are there, eventually they will become visible. The risk of governments doing something sensible follows.

Heavily regulated industries such as aviation, toll roads, healthcare and the salary packaging sector can carry on in damaging ways for decades. When a government finally decides to act, the value of such businesses can fall in an instant. All regulated sectors carry this risk, and the more nothing changes, the more that risk is discounted. Governments can do sensible stuff. Occasionally, they do.

3. Debt is a killer

If you've ever invested in a company that has gone under, debt is likely one of the causes, probably *the* cause. Leverage, as it is known, is a company killer. If you invest only in debt-free companies, your chances of suffering a substantial loss are greatly reduced.

Debt didn't kill Star, but via two huge capital raisings, it killed the investment case for it. Some debt is okay, but the greater the level of gearing, the greater the risk to investors. We must be confident that even in the worst case, the cash flows needed to service the debt will be maintained. Without that, crushing capital raises will destroy the value of your stake.

4. Culture eats strategy for breakfast

Had Star's culture been addressed, the second NSW inquiry – whilst the company was under a special manager – would not have been necessary. Each chance the company got to prove it had changed was met with ineptitude and overconfidence. If you find one cockroach in the kitchen, there are usually more. Take notice of the first rather than waiting for the kitchen to be overrun.

Aftermath

Star has become a corporate synonym for arrogance, incompetence and blinding self-interest. Acclimated to an environment where it could do what it wanted without consequence, when the truth about its operations was finally revealed it preferred to blame others than take responsibility. The result has been like a laugh-free episode of *Blankety Blanks*, where a new CEO is despatched for their idiocy after wrongly guessing their first answer. Truly, it has been a procession of clowns.

The company was culpable and utterly unprepared for the inquiries, legal proceedings, tax increases, mega-fines, capacity limits and regulatory changes that followed. Whilst governments seemed hellbent on squeezing Star in a classic case of overreaction, unlike Walter Summerford's bad luck, Star got what it deserved, plus a bit more. Had anyone at the company accepted its wrongdoing and taken responsibility to correct it, maybe the NSW Government wouldn't have gone in so hard. Star will be a business school case study about how to do everything wrong and keep doing it.

As for our attitude to casinos as an investment, that has not changed. Star's Queen's Wharf development may well turn out to be an excellent asset, but with the debt and the potential loss of its Sydney licence hanging over the company, we won't be going near it for quite a while.

REFERENCES

- 16 Mar 2020: Star & Crown: betting on the long term (intelligentinvestor.com.au/recommendations/star-and-crown-betting-on-the-long-term/147026)
- 17 Apr 2020: Crown and Star get their lifelines (intelligentinvestor.com.au/recommendations/crown-and-star-get-their-lifelines/147261)
- 20 Aug 2020: 2020 result (intelligentinvestor.com.au/recommendations/crown-and-star-results-2020/148464)
- 19 Feb 2021: Interim result 2021 (intelligentinvestor.com.au/recommendations/crown-and-star-interim-results-2021/149404)

- 7 May 2021: Star Entertainment continues to recover (intelligentinvestor.com.au/recommendations/star-entertainment-continues-to-recover/149775)
- 10 May 2021: Crown gets two acquisition proposals (intelligentinvestor.com.au/recommendations/crown-gets-two-acquisition-proposals/149783)
- 23 July 2021: Star withdraws Crown merger proposal (intelligentinvestor.com.au/recommendations/star-withdraws-crown-merger-proposal/150162)
- 20 Aug 2021: Result 2021 (intelligentinvestor.com.au/recommendations/star-entertainment-result-2021/150301)
- 11 Oct 2021: Star Entertainment in the sin bin (intelligentinvestor.com.au/recommendations/star-entertainment-in-the-sin-bin/150547)
- 18 Feb 2022: Interim result 2022 (intelligentinvestor.com.au/recommendations/crown-and-star-interim-results-2022/150972)
- 29 Mar 2022: Star Entertainment's chief (finally) resigns (intelligentinvestor.com.au/recommendations/star-entertainments-chief-finally-resigns/151128)
- 8 Jun 2022: Star Entertainment: bumps and bonuses (intelligentinvestor.com.au/recommendations/star-entertainment-bumps-and-bonuses/151366)
- 14 Sep 2022: Star unfit to run a casino (intelligentinvestor.com.au/recommendations/star-entertainment-unfit-to-run-a-casino/151719)
- 18 Oct 2022: Star gets away with it (intelligentinvestor.com.au/recommendations/star-gets-away-with-it/151838)
- 12 Dec 2022: Queensland fines Star $100m (intelligentinvestor.com.au/recommendations/queensland-fines-star-entertainment-100m/152035)
- 24 Feb 2023: Star jumps the gun (intelligentinvestor.com.au/recommendations/star-jumps-the-gun/152234)
- 20 Apr 2023: Star Entertainment's dimming forecast (intelligentinvestor.com.au/recommendations/star-entertainments-dimming-forecast/152435)
- 11 Aug 2023: Star gets some breathing room (intelligentinvestor.com.au/recommendations/star-entertainment-gets-some-breathing-room/152803)
- 31 Aug 2023: Result 2023 (intelligentinvestor.com.au/recommendations/star-entertainment-result-2023/152876)
- 26 Sep 2023: Star: déjà vu all over again (intelligentinvestor.com.au/recommendations/star-entertainment-deja-vu-all-over-again/152947)
- 20 Feb 2024: Star prodded one last time (intelligentinvestor.com.au/recommendations/star-entertainment-prodded-one-last-time/153309)

Key takeaways from the stocks we sold too late

Economist John Maynard Keynes is credited with saying, 'When the facts change, I change my mind. What do you do, sir?' Keynes, I suspect, knew the answer. In most cases, when facts arise that contradict a view already formed, minds do not change. Confirmation bias is the primary reason for it. Learning how to overcome it is key to reducing losses in stocks that aren't working out.

Adhering to strict portfolio limits is a way of limiting such losses (and gains) for investors who struggle with it, as are more matter-of-fact considerations such as avoiding charismatic leaders, inept or untrustworthy management, and companies overburdened with debt.

Debt is crucial; if a company fails, it is usually because of it. And if there is one cockroach in the kitchen, there are probably more. Do not wait for them to reveal themselves to confirm this truth. If you are going to panic, it is better to do so early. If you invest in a company with a sturdy and enduring business model, you will encounter fewer such problems.

Do not invest in companies that lack capable, trustworthy managers. Energy and intelligence should be a given. What matters most is their ethics. Can they be trusted? Are they respectful to subordinates? Do they admit their mistakes? Are they motivated by the challenge or the money? Do they obfuscate when asked a difficult question? These are questions of character. Managers who lack integrity will use their energy and intelligence against you. They are best avoided.

Also avoid companies that are heavily reliant on a small number of suppliers or are expanding into areas where they have little expertise and experience. Think carefully about regulatory risk. Usually, nothing will happen, but when the media spotlight falls upon them, governments and bureaucrats will sometimes do something sensible.

Finally, there is no substitute for expertise and research. Things can and will go wrong, even for those on the inside playing with smart money. We can all fall victim to tightly held beliefs. If you want to improve, learn from your failures and those of others. Unfortunately, there is no other way, and sometimes the lessons will be expensive.

Part II
Stocks We Sold
Too Soon

Ronald Wayne was the Ringo Starr of Apple Computer Company. Less talented than Steve Jobs or Steve Wozniak, the Lennon and McCartney of personal computers, he was vital to their eventual success. But whilst every Beatle made it to stardom, and Jobs and Wozniak became billionaires, Ronald Wayne was last reported selling stamps to supplement his pension.[1] Wayne got his shot at fame and riches, and he blew it.

Born in 1934, Wayne trained as a technical draughtsman. His first business was designing and making slot machines. After it failed, in 1973 Wayne joined pioneering videogame company Atari. There he met two prototypical computer nerds – the young Steve Jobs and Steve Wozniak. During their regular heated exchanges, Wayne, the self-described 'adult in the room', would mediate.

It was a role in which he excelled. At Wayne's home in April 1975, Jobs and Wozniak agreed to establish Apple Computer Company. Wayne wrote up the partnership agreement on the spot, confirming that each Steve would get 45 percent and himself the remaining 10 percent. When there was a difference of opinion, Wayne would have the casting vote. His role as trusted arbitrator was confirmed.

Young, inexperienced founders are prone to rashness and overconfidence. Even so, they generally do not hand power to a fool. Wayne, having designed the first Apple logo and written the initial *Apple-1 Operation Manual*, was far from a fool. And yet a mere 12 days after signing the agreement, Wayne got out. 'I was getting too old,' he said when later reflecting on his decision, 'and those two were whirlwinds. It was like having a tiger by the tail, and I couldn't keep up.'

---

1   telegraph.co.uk/technology/apple/7624539/US-pensioner-Ronald-Wayne-gave-up-15bn-slice-of-Apple.html

Less than two weeks after becoming a founding partner of what would become one of the world's most successful and profitable companies – featured in this part of the book – Wayne sold his stake for US$1,500. And he did so in the knowledge that the company would probably go on to enjoy some success. Today, even after dilution, that stake would be worth around US$75 billion.

Wayne departed before the curtain went up, unaware that his life would be remembered mainly for what he missed out on. After leaving Atari, he opened a stamp shop. After multiple burglaries, he continued the business from home. In 2010, newspaper reports suggested he was still selling stamps to supplement his pension.

Warren Buffett said, 'If you find three wonderful businesses in your life, you'll get very rich'. Wayne found just one that would have done the job, and he let it slip. He is in good company. Every investor has their Ronald Wayne moments. Part II examines ours, explaining what happened, why it happened and what we learned from the ones that got away. These may not be the most emotionally scarring errors, but they were the costliest.

Wayne, for his part, never regretted selling his Apple shares, recognising that he didn't want to bear the risk they entailed. As he told Nick Allen, a reporter for the UK's *The Telegraph*, 'Everybody would like to be rich, but I couldn't keep up the pace. I would have been wealthy, but I would have been the richest man in the cemetery'. Some years after he exited the partnership, Jobs tried to re-hire him, but he refused.

A $10,000 investment in Apple in early 1981 would now be worth $20 million (accounting for splits and dividends). The decisions made and not made along the way need not leave you in the cemetery, as Wayne feared. If you can learn to sit still and do nothing, you will have conquered much of the challenge.

There are untold ways to improve as an investor. I'd suggest you first concentrate your efforts on the Ronald Wayne moments and learn from the mistakes of others. This is less expensive than personal experience and heaps more fun. Here is our contribution.

Case Study #4
Cochlear
Cutting the prettiest flower

Wipe-outs hurt, but there is an investment mistake more painful and costly. Cutting a successful investment off at the knees aches far more than incurring the losses on stocks such as Star Entertainment and Roc Oil. Welcome to our most expensive mistake of all.

What happened

Australia has few world-class businesses. Our geology and climate have nurtured impressive companies in resources and agriculture, but those born of human ingenuity alone are less common. The healthcare industry provides some exceptions; Australia has created a string of globally successful health-related businesses. Some have become ten baggers. A few have then gone on to become hundred baggers. Pioneering hearing-implant company Cochlear is one of them.

From an early age, Graeme Clark wanted to 'fix ears'[1]; having watched his father suffer from hearing loss, he wanted to help people with similar conditions. Embarking on a medical career, Clark

---

[1]   amazon.co.uk/Want-Fix-Ears-Cochlear-Implant/dp/0645067105

specialised in ear, nose and throat surgery, eventually theorising that deafness might be overcome if electrical stimulation of the auditory nerve could mimic the functioning of a healthy inner ear (or cochlea).

In 1977, Clark was holidaying on Minnamurra Beach[2], half an hour south of Wollongong, New South Wales. Strolling along the sand, he came across a turban shell. Noticing the similarities in its structure to the inner ear, he poked a blade of grass into it. It was a eureka moment. Maybe, wondered Clark, there was a way to insert wires into the cochlea. Clark didn't invent the initial implant that replicated the role of the auditory nerve, but he was the first to use a multi-channel device. In 1978, Rod Saunders, after losing his hearing in a car accident, was its first recipient.[3]

Cochlear, founded in 1981 as a subsidiary of medical electronics company Nucleus to promote Clark's invention, now leads the world in this field. Over 750,000 Cochlear implants and processors have been installed globally.[4] The current cost of a single unit is around $30,000.[5] The company's bone-anchored hearing aids (BAHAs), which can address single-sided deafness and mixed hearing loss, cost around $10,000. Further revenue comes from processor upgrades and other services.

After being acquired by Pacific Dunlop in 1988, Cochlear listed on the ASX in 1995 as a part of that company's break-up. The original offer price was $2.50.[6] The company now operates in over 30 countries. At the time of writing, it trades at around $330 a share.

In the investing world, this is what a pioneer species looks like. No matter what mistakes you make elsewhere, a 1,200 percent increase over almost 30 years will more than offset the damage. If, in your investing life, you can find two or three companies like this and hang on – subject to maintaining sensible portfolio limits – you should do

---

2   sydney.edu.au/news-opinion/news/2017/04/06/sound-with-vision.html
3   family-news.cochlear.com/en-uk/inspiring-generations/
4   www.ncbi.nlm.nih.gov/pmc/articles/PMC8476711/
5   clarityhearingsolutions.com.au/implants/hearing-implant-pricing/
6   intelligentinvestor.com.au/shares/asx-coh/cochlear-limited/float

just fine. As we shall see, identifying Australia's best businesses is easy. Buying them at reasonable prices and hanging on is the hard part.

Over the past 25 years, including all buys, sells and holds, *Intelligent Investor* has made over 100 recommendations on Cochlear. Four are worthy of scrutiny.

The first was in mid-1998. After winning U.S. Food and Drug Administration approval, Cochlear joined the buy list at a price of $6.30.

The second occurred less than four years later. In early 2002, we sold out at $41.40, recognising a gain of over 500 percent. The sale reflected our view that the share price had risen beyond its intrinsic value and that we'd like to own the company again 'at the right price'. The timing was fortuitous. A string of sell and hold recommendations followed, accompanied by a falling stock price. Cochlear was facing growing competition in the US, and many states were cutting health budgets.

In late 2003, Cochlear issued a profit warning and the stock dived 27 percent in a few days. The price was now right. We made our third major call. At a price of $20.70, Cochlear was back on the buy list at half the price we had sold it for less than two years earlier. It couldn't have worked out better had we planned it.

There followed over a decade of hanging on, which is harder than it sounds. Cochlear was at the top of its game, growing sales and profits. Having bought well, we were happy to hold. By late 2014, Cochlear's share price was heading towards $70. It had taken longer than during our first period of ownership, but things were working out as they had between 1998 and 2002.

After getting the first three major decisions right, the fourth was our undoing. In early 2015, company results showed upgrade sales doubling but unit sales falling. With inflexible fixed manufacturing costs, lower sales had crushed margins. Net profit was down 75 percent. With little margin of safety, Cochlear looked overpriced. We recommended members sell at $86.08, hoping to buy back in once the market had absorbed the extent of the problems and the share price had reacted accordingly. Unfortunately, that chance never came.

Nevertheless, over our two periods of ownership, beginning in late 2003 and ending in 2015, Cochlear had returned a little over 2,600 percent at a compound annual growth rate (CAGR) of 25 percent. Who could possibly complain about that? Well, those who examined potential returns had we made one decision rather than four might. If we had simply purchased Cochlear at $6.30 a share in mid-1998 and done nothing, in February 2024 our return would have been about 4,460 percent (see Figure 5). Including dividends, it would be more. This is the value of doing nothing.

Figure 5: Cochlear's share price since 1 December 1995

As usual in investing, there is a caveat. Whilst the CAGR from our two periods of ownership was over 25 percent, had we simply purchased Cochlear in 1998 and held on until February 2024, despite the much higher overall return, the CAGR would fall to just over 16 percent.

For someone like Warren Buffett, who finds investments that compound at over 25 percent a year with depressing regularity, our real-life experience would be preferential. From the time of our second purchase, Cochlear experienced a lower CAGR of 14 percent. Buffett could probably get more than that elsewhere. But most people are not Warren Buffett, us included. Once one accepts that mundane but unarguable premise, a 16 percent annual return over a quarter century should be viewed as exceptional.

While a 2,600 percent return over 15 years at a CAGR of 25 percent is good, a 4,460 percent return over 25 years at a lower CAGR of 16 percent would have been better. There is an old saying that you 'never go broke taking a profit'. Our first purchase and disposal of Cochlear verifies this truth. There is another old saying that 'selling your winners is like cutting the best flowers from your garden'. Despite making 27 times our initial investment, we had also cut the best flower in the garden.

Why it happened

To cut the prettiest flower in our portfolio required three simple steps. The first was analytical, which opened to the door to two more psychological factors that facilitated the error.

1. We underestimated intrinsic value

Every calculation an investor makes occurs at a point in time. Value investors ascribe a numerical value to things such as intellectual property rights, brand power and investment in research and development by establishing a current value of future sales and profit margins. The problem is that small changes in these metrics, and things like interest rates, can produce big changes in estimates of current value.

The further one looks into the future, the greater the impact of small changes. At the time of the sale, we didn't underestimate Cochlear's intrinsic value by much, but over time the company grew faster and more profitably than we anticipated. Those small differences had a big impact on future value. Having consistently underestimated Cochlear's earnings power, the result was that many of our 'sell' recommendations after 2015 should have been 'holds', and many of the 'holds' should have been 'buys'.

2. We were too anchored on price and value

Investors are emotional. We can be as enthusiastic as Swifties at Taylor's first gig in years or as depressed as flat-earthers looking at the planet from a window inside the International Space Station. Value investors aim to take advantage of this bipolarity, buying into pessimism and selling into overexcitement. The difference between the intrinsic value of a stock and the price at which it trades is a loose proxy for this sentiment. The bigger the gap, the stronger the case to buy or sell.

The tools for assessing intrinsic value – usually a spreadsheet and a discounted cash flow (DCF) analysis – are useful but also contain a trap. Producing a DCF brings with it the risk of becoming pre-committed to the numbers in it. With Cochlear, we were anchored on our estimate of intrinsic value, underestimating its ability to grow. Among Australia's best businesses, this is a common mistake, as this section proves.

3. We were overconfident

Almost everything in this book is loaded with hindsight bias. That our initial success made us overconfident is one of many examples. Making a 557 percent return between 1998 and 2002 didn't help our goal of maximising future returns despite the stunning figure. Had we not timed our first entry and exit perfectly, we might have been more willing to hang on. Overconfidence is one reason we did not. As a result, one of the best companies in Australia hasn't been on the buy list in a decade.

Lessons

Here are the lessons we learned from investing in Cochlear.

1. Buy good businesses going through tough times

Poor businesses tend to deliver nasty surprises; good businesses tend to surprise well. Occasionally, though, something goes wrong. This is often the best time to buy, with Cochlear the perfect example.

In late 2003, a profit warning produced a 25 percent share price fall in a few days. Between late 2007 and mid-2008, the peak of the financial crisis, the share price halved. Between April and October 2011, after a product recall, it did so again. And in the early stages of the pandemic the share price fell almost 40 percent in five weeks. These are the times to be brave in the face of fear.

2. It's worth paying up for quality

Quality is easily recognised, which is why the best companies rarely trade at cheap prices. Even when they stumble, investors generally recognise their ability to quickly recover. This is the price of quality. Usually, it is worth paying for. It is better to own a great business purchased at a reasonable price than a poor one purchased cheaply only to watch it become cheaper still.

3. Hang on, preferably forever

High-quality companies compound and grow at a faster rate than most investors can achieve themselves. If a company like Cochlear can invest, say, an additional $10,000 in its business and get a better return on it than you are likely to yourself, make life easy and let them do it.

4. High portfolio turnover equals poor performance

Trading in and out of stocks is a bit like changing lanes in heavy traffic. We get the sense of improving our situation but rarely the reality. The investment of time and fuel achieves little.

Investors who buy and hold stocks tend to have better performance than those who trade in and out. A US study of 66,000 investors found that those who traded the most lagged behind the overall market's performance by 7 percent.[7] Overconfidence and the long-term effects of higher costs explain why. Brokerage costs and taxes might seem trivial to your portfolio's overall value, but an additional 1 percent a year in costs will reduce your portfolio's value by over a quarter in 30 years' time. Buying and selling regularly is setting the benefits of compounding against you.

If you make fewer decisions and hang on to good businesses, there's every chance you'll beat professional investors who, saddled by short-term performance targets, make more decisions and thus get more wrong. Time is the retail investor's biggest and best advantage.

5. Don't sweat the wipe-outs

The mind lingers on mistakes because the pain of losing $1,000 is greater than the joy of making the same amount. This evolutionary wiring can lead us to miss the bigger picture. Big losses hurt, but they don't matter as much as we think.

Stocks can fall to zero, but they can also rise tenfold or a hundredfold. Profit-taking and topping up aside, as your winners get bigger, your mistakes get smaller. Focus on getting good companies into your portfolio and forget about the disasters. Over the course of 20 years, even randomness will give you a few ten baggers. Your job is to find them and hang on.

Aftermath

Cochlear wasn't the only high-quality business we purchased and let go of too quickly. We have made the same mistake with biotechnology company CSL and Fisher & Paykel Healthcare. As with Cochlear, the intrinsic value of both companies grew faster than we expected. This was proof that we let go of them too easily.

---

7   http://faculty.haas.berkeley.edu/odean/papers%20current%20versions/individual_investor_performance_final.pdf

There are good psychological reasons for doing so. Humans have a bias towards activity. We have come to dominate the planet because doing *something* is an assertion of our existence, an act that psychologists call 'self-actualisation'. Doing the opposite – nothing – is a denial of it.

This complicates investing. If day trading is an expression of being frantically alive, those holding a stock purchased 20 years ago might feel a kind of existence-denial. We need to get over this. Becoming intimately familiar with a business and exercising that knowledge by *not* doing something with it is difficult. But choosing to do nothing *is* doing something, especially with regards to Australia's best businesses (see Appendix).

It took us a while to learn this lesson, but we are getting better at doing nothing. Sitting still is hard, but if we are to let the best flowers in the garden grow, we must learn how to do nothing.

REFERENCES

· 3 July 1998: Cochlear upgraded (intelligentinvestor.com.au/recommendations/cochlear-limited/47235)

· 30 Jul 2002: Take profits on Cochlear (intelligentinvestor.com.au/recommendations/cochlear-limited/50871)

· 17 Dec 2003: Cochlear upgraded (intelligentinvestor.com.au/recommendations/cochlear-limited/53242)

· 11 Feb 2015: Interim result 2015 (intelligentinvestor.com.au/recommendations/cochlear-interim-result-2015/60823)

Case Study #5
ARB Corp
Dropping the bull

ARB was everything we look for in a successful investment: it was a market leader, its founder had skin in the game, and it had great products and a growing market. With a stunning financial performance over decades, we underestimated the impacts of each of these qualities.

What happened

In the midwinter of 2004, an *Intelligent Investor* analyst took a holiday in Victoria. Having spent months researching ARB Corp, a manufacturer and distributor of four-wheel drive (4WD) components, he made a side trip to the company's headquarters in Melbourne's outer suburbs.

The building was a daggy, low-rent affair plonked next to a car park stuffed with filthy off-road vehicles. Inside, the carpets were threadbare, the filing cabinets ancient and the desks busted. He was impressed. This was not a profitless company with a founder who spent $400,000 on a vanity car to be paraded on Instagram. If the old saying 'the thicker the carpet, the thinner the dividend' held any weight, he thought, this might be a winner.

In 1975, founder Tony Brown took an expedition to Cape York. At the time, 4WD drivers were either tinkerers, building their own bull bars and roof racks in the garden shed, or suckers, purchasing low-quality products that broke as soon as they hit corrugation. Brown returned with the idea of a company that made well-engineered, durable equipment for 4WD owners.

Taking the initials of his name as inspiration, Brown worked in the family garage to try out his ideas. Recognising the opportunity, he started ARB, bringing his two brothers, Andrew and Roger, on board. ARB took the best aspects of a family business and avoided the worst. The company is now Australia's largest manufacturer and distributor of 4WD accessories, exporting to over 100 countries.[1] Locally, the company operates about 60 ARB-branded stores. ARB is an enduring global success story. Andrew Brown remains its managing director while brother Roger chairs the board.

ARB is a company of enthusiasts, acting as much from passion as pay cheque. Salaries are modest and executive options are non-existent. At the 2002 annual meeting, so the story goes, Roger took the leftover sandwiches back to the office for the staff's enjoyment.

As with Cochlear, ARB also invested heavily in research and development. According to a company profile, management's adage is that 'if it's not broken, break it anyway and find a better way of making it'. ARB had a few hits in its early years, including the Air Locker and Old Man Emu suspension kits – the first 4WD accessory to sound like a boutique beer. The company's expertise and experience meant the chances of more hits were high. The products on its website are an indication of the loyalty it inspires. ARB-branded umbrellas available for $39 imply brand power, but $29 for a pair of ARB Off-Road Socks (normal socks with added dust?) suggests religious-style devotion.

---

1   ibisworld.com/au/company/arb-corporation-limited/3445/

ARB was an enticing investment prospect. Good management kept manufacturing costs down, high levels of investment produced great products, and the company's market niche was a large and growing pool of aficionados prepared to pay top dollar for everything from bull bars to stubby holders. The result was an EBIT (earnings before interest and taxes) margin consistently above 15 percent, more than twice that of its nearest competitor. The attention to detail and careful management evident in ARB's products were also on display in its finances. Over the ten years to 2003, ARB had increased profits by an average of 29 percent a year. Return on equity, then about 26 percent, had grown in the previous five years.

ARB ticked every box in the owner/manager matrix, including high insider ownership, founder involvement in day-to-day management, a lucrative niche and an established, well-managed and growing brand. The problem was the price. In October 2003, at a price earnings ratio (PER) of 20 and with an uninspiring yield, we could only manage a hold recommendation.

Then, in mid-2004, we bit the bullet, calling ARB a long-term buy at $3.53. Having recognised the company's quality, we were willing to pay for it. Our confidence was immediately tested when the stock suffered a 25 percent loss over the next 18 months. Having done the work, we continued to recommend buying. A recovery above $4 followed, but the stock again fell below $3 during the 2008 global financial crisis (GFC). That proved to be the best buying opportunity in 20 years. During the pandemic, the share price breached $50 before resuming its pre-COVID-19 trend. In mid-2024, ARB's shares were changing hands at over $38.

That would have made our initial recommendation two decades before a ten bagger. Sadly, it wasn't to be. In early 2013, ARB's share price had climbed to $13.49, having met all our expectations and then some. At a multiple of 22 times that year's earnings, we baulked. Fretting about the potential fallout from the then-looming mining bust, we made our solitary sell recommendation and removed the stock from our model growth portfolio.

Over the decade we owned it, ARB had delivered an annual return of just under 17 percent (or a few percent more including dividends). It hasn't quite matched that in the decade since, but the 10 percent a year it has delivered (again, plus dividends) is around double that of the All Ordinaries index. By hanging on, we could have maintained our market-beating return, made fewer decisions, saved on transaction costs and delayed a tax bill. Like Cochlear, this was another great stock we let slip.

Why it happened

There's a feeling you get when you successfully sell a good business. Banking a big profit, textbook-style as with ARB, is energising. That satisfaction is tempered by the fear you're letting a good business go too cheaply. Maybe this is the cost of selling a great business – the constant reminder that hanging on was probably best.

The reasons for selling ARB had nothing to do with the business and everything to do with the price. Having bought cheaply, as value investors are primed to do, we thought we were selling at a reasonable price. This is no bad thing. But it does entail the risk of underestimating ARB's ability to continue to grow and generate profits. That is what transpired. Furthermore, during the pandemic lows in March 2020, we had the chance to buy back in and, busy putting over 30 other stocks on the buy list at the time, missed it.

Once in your portfolio, high-quality companies like ARB that performed well through challenging conditions usually deserve the benefit of the doubt. We were nervous about where the company might find its next leg of growth, but we should simply have kept faith with the company's outstanding owner managers and exceptional culture.

Our experience with Cochlear describes the same circumstances. We underestimated ARB's intrinsic value, were too focused on the price we paid for it and were overconfident. Having seen ARB's stock price fall dramatically a few times, we instinctively thought we'd get the chance to buy in again having sold out at a suitably high price, missing the opportunity to compound our returns for another decade.

Lessons

Here are the lessons we learned from investing in ARB.

1. You will have to learn the same lesson more than once

The human brain is not easily reprogrammed. As advertisers know, information only penetrates with repetition. You will likely need to make multiple similar mistakes before grasping the lesson they are communicating.

ARB and Cochlear were enough in our case, but these experiences have only reduced our risk of selling out too early rather than eliminating it entirely. It will probably be the same for you. Errors cannot be avoided, but once you have made the same mistake a few times, you will reduce their frequency.

2. Deep research pays off

A cursory look at ARB's annual reports revealed the company's quality. This was more than a low-margin metal-basher. The 'softer' factors were less obvious: the level of commitment among managers, the loyalty of customers and staff, and the quality of its products. It was these, not the high return on equity or profit margin, that got us to a point where we were comfortable paying a seemingly high price for the stock.

It's a mistake to think that everything important can be gleaned from a company's accounts. Deep research must also address the softer side of analysis, the art as much as the science, the sandwiches and the car park. Rich rewards await those who make that commitment.

3. Seek out owner managers

The quote 'Always back the horse named self-interest. It'll be the only one who's trying,' is variously attributed to Paul Keating, Jack Lang, Gough Whitlam and Ben Chifley. Whoever it was, the sentiment captures the benefits of owner managers over the hired help that populate the ASX 200 index.

According to corporate recruiters Robert Half, the average tenure of ASX 200 companies is five years and eight months. Tony Brown started ARB from his garage in 1975 and remains involved. The results speak for themselves. It is better to invest alongside a management team with meaningful stakes in the businesses they run, preferably acquired with their own cash rather than overly generous options grants.

Aftermath

Manufacturing and selling 4WD accessories is inherently less profitable than something as life-changing as a Cochlear implant. It was an obvious mistake to sell Cochlear. With ARB, the error is less clear-cut. Since our sale in 2013, the company has returned on average 10 percent a year plus dividends. It's hardly a disaster to have missed out.

That said, committing to holding ARB – a high-quality, owner-managed business – would have removed the anxiety of having to tackle another sell decision, the hardest decision of all, and then finding another stock where the potential returns were greater and the commensurate risk lower than those of ARB.

This is the value of inactivity, of simply sitting. Once you've found a well-managed, growing company and purchased it at a reasonable price, don't get sucked into thinking there's an even better one just around the corner. Overtrading can ruin your returns, and sometimes the next big thing is the stock you already own.

REFERENCES

- 3 Oct 2003: ARB impresses, price doesn't (intelligentinvestor.com.au/recommendations/arb-impresses-price-doesnand039t/53040)

- 19 Aug 2004: ARB makes tracks (intelligentinvestor.com.au/recommendations/arb-makes-tracks/53862)

- 2 Mar 2005: ARB on a roll (intelligentinvestor.com.au/recommendations/arb-on-a-roll/54242)

- 6 Jul 2005: ARB jumps final hurdle (intelligentinvestor.com.au/recommendations/arb-jumps-the-final-hurdle/54476)

- 30 Aug 2006: Returns from the outback (intelligentinvestor.com.au/recommendations/arb-returns-from-the-outback/55244)

- 30 Jan 2007: Passes mettle test (intelligentinvestor.com.au/recommendations/arb-passes-mettle-test/55609)

- 21 Aug 2008: Determination pays off (intelligentinvestor.com.au/recommendations/arbs-determination-pays-off/56572)

- 19 Aug 2009: ARB bumps the crisis (intelligentinvestor.com.au/recommendations/arb-bumps-the-crisis/57106)

- 6 Nov 2009: Profit upgrade (intelligentinvestor.com.au/recommendations/arb-corp-profit-upgrade/57220)

- 19 Aug 2010: Results do the torquing (intelligentinvestor.com.au/recommendations/arbs-results-do-the-torquing/57710)

- 19 Aug 2011: Two speed-result (intelligentinvestor.com.au/recommendations/arbs-two-speed-result/58434)

- 15 Aug 2012: Result 2012 (intelligentinvestor.com.au/recommendations/arb-corp-result-2012/59096)

- 21 Feb 2013: Interim result 2013 (intelligentinvestor.com.au/recommendations/arb-corp-interim-result-2013/59476)

- 21 May 2013: Selling ARB (intelligentinvestor.com.au/recommendations/arb-corp/59675)

- 4 May 2018: Dreamtime for ARB (intelligentinvestor.com.au/recommendations/dreamtime-for-arb/142563)

Case Study #6
Apple
Crumbled

Wall Street got one of the world's best businesses wrong twice in five years. After making nine times my money, so did I. The decision to sell a good business is the hardest of all. Apple illustrates the difficulties.

What happened

Author's note: at the time of my Apple purchase and sale, Intelligent Investor *did not cover US-listed stocks. This recounts my experience, not that of the business.*

The idea that the explosion of an Indonesian volcano was instrumental to the birth of the bicycle seems implausible. History, via Baron Karl von Drais's biographer, suggests otherwise.

In April 1815, Mount Tambora, in modern-day Indonesia, expelled millions of tons of volcanic ash into the atmosphere.[1] The world went dark, temperatures fell and rainfall increased. As crops failed, food shortages engulfed North America, Europe and China. Unable to pay for oats, farmers in southern Germany shot their horses.

---

1   en.wikipedia.org/wiki/1815_eruption_of_Mount_Tambora

A year later, Baron Karl von Drais invented the draisine.[2] According to his biographer, Hans-Erhard Lessing, his inspiration was to replace horses, many of which had been shot and possibly eaten. Lacking a crank and pedals, the draisine wasn't yet a bicycle, but it was light, commercially successful and didn't eat oats. Six thousand years previously, humanity had invented the wheel. Drais had finally put two of them together and created the precursor to what historian Robert A Smith called 'the freedom machine'.

Steve Jobs once described the computer as a 'bicycle of the mind'. On first holding the iPhone 3GS, I was reminded of those rare occasions when man and machine effortlessly combine. For the first time, I felt the urge to buy Apple stock. It would be four years before I did so.

In the late 1990s, Apple flirted with bankruptcy, rescued only by a Saudi prince and arch-rival Microsoft, which, for regulatory reasons, needed to keep its weak and only competitor alive. Their investments have been incredibly successful. Apple went on to create the iPod and iPhone, both of which I loved. I even bought eight of the original iMacs for *Intelligent Investor* staff.

Despite my adoration of its products, I was less enthralled by Apple stock. I thought of Apple's failures like the Newton, an early stylus-based tablet, and MobileMe, a cloud product that wouldn't sync. I wasn't convinced the iPhone would avoid such a fate.

Wall Street agreed. Matthew Lynn of *Bloomberg* captured the sentiment, describing the iPhone as 'nothing more than a luxury bauble that will appeal to a few gadget freaks'.[3] The mainstream media, eagerly fed by Wall Street analysts, were similarly derisive. It would not be the first time Wall Street got Apple wrong.

After the release of the 3GS, iPhone sales exploded. Apple's stock price followed, quadrupling between mid-2009 and late 2012.[4] If you

---

2   en.wikipedia.org/wiki/Draisine
3   macdailynews.com/2007/01/15/bloomberg_writer_apple_iphone_wont_make_long_term_mark/
4   statista.com/statistics/519699/iphone-sales-by-model-worldwide/

want to change the consensus in financial markets, a fourfold increase in share price is the ideal way to go about it. Wall Street climbed aboard the new bicycle of the mind. By September 2012, of the 39 rated analysts that covered Apple, 38 thought it a buy.[5] The herd had turned, and Apple was in favour.

Then it turned again. Apple was now making too much money. Apple's margins, said Wall Street analysts, were too high, and sales of Android phones would bring them down just as personal Windows computers had overwhelmed Macs in the 1990s. Without Steve Jobs, who had died in 2011, the argument went that Apple 'was dead in the water' and 'running out of juice'.[6]

By the time of my first purchase in mid-2013 – at a price of $432.19, or $15.44 after adjusting for subsequent stock splits – the uniformity of thinking, the misunderstanding of Apple's culture and an inability to differentiate between a physical device and the transformative experience it might deliver left Apple growing like Topsy and trading on a single-digit PER. What was to become one of the world's best businesses was unbelievably cheap. I planted the flower in my garden.

Famed 1980s fund manager Peter Lynch said it was best to invest in something you know. I thought my knowledge of Apple's products, its history and culture gave me an edge. Over the next eight years, Apple became a 'nine bagger' for me. And yet some of the views of Wall Street analysts were vindicated: Android did become the most popular phone operating system, prices did fall and Apple did lose market share.

What they got wrong was the company's ability to retain valuable consumers and charge them higher prices. Android took most of the market; Apple took most of the profits.

Then in 2021, eight years after I had planted Apple stock in my portfolio, I pulled it up and sold out at US$139.96 – just over nine times my purchase price. Warren Buffett, meanwhile, had first

5   eu.usatoday.com/story/money/markets/2012/10/09/apple-stock-must-own/1609157/
6   theguardian.com/commentisfree/2013/mar/09/debate-apple-out-of-juice

purchased shares in Apple in 2016 and has held on since. At the time of writing, Apple is trading at around US$195. Had I followed in Buffett's footsteps, my ninefold gain would have been twelvefold.

Why it happened

There are three principal reasons why I failed to maximise my Apple gains.

1. Sentiment changed

In mid-2018, Apple became the first company to pass US$1 trillion by market capitalisation. By mid-2023, that figure had reached US$3 trillion. Could Apple really be worth three times more than five years previously? Well, it had an impregnable global fortress built upon almost 1.5 billion active iPhones, 2 billion Apple devices and billions of engaged customers, but this had long been the case. I may have underestimated Apple's intrinsic value in 2021, as we did with Cochlear, but a change in market sentiment is a more likely cause.

If you're looking for stocks that triple in a few years, the largest companies in the world are not usually the place to find them. What had changed was not so much Apple's intrinsic value but investors' perceptions of it. During the pandemic, the price of technology stocks rocketed. As normality resumed and interest rates started to increase, the giants of Silicon Valley were perceived as safe havens. The S&P 500 is now dominated by the so-called Magnificent Seven of Apple, Alphabet, Amazon, Meta, Microsoft, Nvidia and Tesla. Sentiment had transformed the perceptions and valuations of these companies, Apple included, twice in a decade.

2. The media promoted popularity over accuracy

The Internet has changed the media landscape. A commitment to accuracy is no longer rewarded as much as emotive opinion, often poorly argued. Coverage of Apple makes the point. Analysts and commentators got more attention for bold, headline-grabbing predictions, usually concerning Apple's demise, than nuanced research. In business journalism, as elsewhere, the bias is toward popularity over accuracy.

This contributed to Apple's share price fall in late 2012 and early 2013. Inaccurate, hyperbolic media coverage caused many Apple shareholders to offload their stock. That gave me the opportunity to buy. The reverse – a slavish reporting of Apple's financial brilliance – contributed to the rise since I sold out.

3. Risks were discounted

At the time of my sale, Apple was performing perfectly. Lengthening iPhone upgrade cycles were offset by price rises and a booming services business. Products such as AirPods and the Apple Watch were strengthening the lock on Apple customers. The quality of the company's products was not in doubt.

The political environment, however, was deteriorating. In 2018, Australia banned Huawei, a global leader in mobile infrastructure technology, from the rollout of our 5G networks.[7] Other countries followed, kneecapping one of China's biggest technology-led export companies. The bans were not imposed in isolation. In early 2018, US President Donald Trump enacted trade barriers and tariffs against China, which then took retaliatory action.[8]

No company was more exposed than Apple. Apple chief executive Tim Cook had been the architect of a supply chain that had China at its core. Subcontracted manufacturers such as Foxconn supplied 95 percent of all Apple devices. Without China, Apple wouldn't and couldn't be Apple. This was true of demand as much as it was supply. In 2021, China accounted for about a third of global Apple sales. If it chose to, China could wreck Apple's business. In the midst of a trade war, the company had a giant target on its back.

---

7 smh.com.au/technology/government-implies-5g-china-ban-in-new-security-advice-20180823-p4zz77.html
8 reuters.com/article/idUSKBN1ZE1AA/

Investor enthusiasm for Apple had pushed its price well beyond my estimate of intrinsic value. In the background was the huge risk of retaliatory action by the Chinese government, which could diminish Apple's capacity to grow into the price investors ascribed to it. This was a risk Warren Buffett was prepared to take and I was not. So far, he has been proved right.

Lessons

Here are the lessons I learned from investing in Apple.

1. Market share is a poor guide to profit

In 2012, sales of Samsung's Galaxy mobile phone exploded. Echoing the historical parallel of Microsoft colonising the market for PCs at Apple's expense, there was a widespread view that Samsung's top-line but cheaper product would crush Apple's.

Data supported this view. In the fourth quarter of 2011, Apple and Samsung each had 24 percent of the smartphone market.[9] Within two years, Apple's share had almost halved whilst Samsung's had increased to 31 percent.[10] Analysts assumed Apple's declining market share would lead to lower profitability. Instead, its far smaller global market share captured 70 to 80 percent of the profits in the smartphone sector.[11]

Market share matters more in commoditised markets than in high-profit-margin, brand-driven markets, where higher market shares can undermine profit margins. Apple products, highly priced and highly prized, aren't commodities. In these areas, market share is less significant than profit margins.

---

9   commsbusiness.co.uk/content/news/gartner-says-worldwide-smartphone-sales-
     soared-in-4q11/
10 gartner.com/en/newsroom/press-releases/2014-02-13-gartner-says-annual-smartphone-
     sales-surpassed-sales-of-feature-phones-for-the-first-time-in-2013
11 latimes.com/business/la-xpm-2013-jan-31-la-fi-tn-apple-samsung-95-percent-global-
     phone-profits-20130131-story.html

2. Numbers are not enough

After the death of Steve Jobs, many analysts predicted Apple would enter a long decline. This fundamentally misunderstood his endeavours. Walter Isaacson's biography *Steve Jobs* made it clear that Jobs wanted Apple to endure and prosper after his death.

Operating at the intersection of technology and the liberal arts, Apple's culture was humanistic rather than utilitarian. This is why its products feel right. This insight was critical to understanding the company but could not be gleaned from financial models or hard data. It took Wall Street analysts a decade to understand because it couldn't be written into a spreadsheet. Numbers alone are not enough.

3. Some companies are rule breakers

There are a lot of unwritten rules in business. The law of large numbers, for example, says that big companies cannot grow at the same pace as small ones, that eventually every market becomes commoditised, and that the businesses that win the market share battle make the most money. These are good analytical guides, but every now and again a company comes along and rips them up. Apple is one such example.

Because most investors, analysts and commentators implicitly accept these rules, they find it difficult to spot where they don't apply. Investors prepared to look through the mist and consider the possibility of rule breakers can find wonderful opportunities.

4. Politics doesn't matter until it does

Another gem from Peter Lynch, oft quoted by value investors, is, 'If you spend 13 minutes a year on economics, you've wasted 10 minutes.'[12] Lynch was right. It's generally better to focus on understanding a business than the economic and political environments in which it operates.

---

12 pbs.org/wgbh/pages/frontline/shows/betting/pros/lynch.html

Occasionally, though, external risks can become acute and deserve consideration. Apple hasn't yet been engulfed by a trade war but, recognising the risk, it's desperately moving manufacturing away from China into countries such as Vietnam and India. Serendipitous, at least for China, this is not. As its importance to the Chinese economy diminishes, the risk of punitive action increases.

In late 2023, for example, China reportedly banned work iPhone use among government officials and state-owned enterprises.[13] This coincided with the release of an iPhone competitor from Huawei, the Mate 60 Pro. The risk of retaliation has increased because the politics is worsening.

Frustrating as it has been to miss out on making twelve rather than nine times my money, I don't look back on the 2021 sale as an error. The subsequent price increase is not in itself evidence of a poor decision. Apple is not Cochlear; it faces political risks that Cochlear does not. To disregard them might look like a mistake in hindsight, but with context it may not be. I would have liked to own Apple forever, but politics stopped me from doing so. Usually, politics doesn't matter. Occasionally, nothing matters more.

5. You won't get the timing right

Had I held on a little longer, I would have required more good luck to successfully forecast Apple's future intrinsic value and future sentiment towards it. It is one thing to work out what you think a stock is worth and quite another to establish what other people think it is worth.

This is what timing a stock purchase or sale demands. It is an unproductive task. That anyone can assess what is in the heads of other investors when many of them do not know themselves seems implausible. Successfully picking the best time to buy or sell a stock is an illusion, and those that manage to do it mistake luck for skill.

---

13   wsj.com/world/china/china-bans-iphone-use-for-government-officials-at-work-635fe2f8

I may have got my timing 'wrong' on my Apple sale, but that is to be expected. It is best not to beat yourself up about missing out on further gains, especially when the risks that prompted the sale were real.

6. Narratives change, opportunities return

Many investors now view Apple as impregnable. Some also believe China has become 'uninvestable'. These two conflicting narratives promoted in broker reports and the mainstream media exist simultaneously, demonstrating their effortless inconsistencies.

Such narratives can change, as Apple's did a decade ago. If its valuation tumbles after China does to it what the West did to Huawei, I might get another chance to buy back in. For now, I'm watching from the sidelines, awaiting the draisine-like sense of freedom and joy from whatever Cupertino dreams up next.

Aftermath

Apple might seem a minor error, but for a long time it didn't feel that way. All I had to do to add another third to my returns was, like Buffett, nothing. With hindsight, I felt at first that my decision to sell Apple in 2021 was foolish and arrogant.

As the years passed, I came to see this as a superficial analysis. I have included this case study as it illustrates that not everything in investing is clear-cut, and it's difficult to get the sell decision right – so difficult, in fact, that sometimes you don't really know whether you have blundered or not.

Knowing now that I could have made more by hanging on influences my recollection of past events and information. This is what hindsight bias does. It irons out complexity, diminishes emotion and ransacks valid arguments to make everything about the past clear and obvious in the present. The initial effect was to make me feel more foolish than I really was. China could have retaliated against the United States by making life difficult for Apple (and it still may). Warren Buffett might have been wrong, and I might have been proved right.

Instead, I took my healthy Apple profits and had the opportunity to invest them elsewhere without bearing the existential risk of a trade war. I sold a globe-straddling compounder to do so but, accounting for hindsight bias, do not consider it a mistake in the manner of Cochlear or ARB.

There is a lot of emotional baggage involved in selling compared with buying. When buying a stock, a seductive future beckons, not yet sullied by terrible managers, disappointing results and the rude interruption of reality. The possibilities are exciting precisely because they haven't yet happened. When selling, the future is behind us. The baggage is often the only thing left.

Questions like these play on our minds, twisting our synapses, eroding our capacity for sensible decision-making. What seems obvious when emotions are running hot usually isn't. It takes costly raw experience to learn that markets eventually recover. It also takes a dash of overconfidence to believe you can sell now and buy back in at a lower price later.

High-quality businesses usually emerge from difficult periods in good shape and their share prices recover, often more quickly than you'd imagine. Sometimes, though, it can take years, which is why we need to be prepared to wait it out, letting history unfold in our favour rather than trying to write our own (potentially costly) version of it. And sometimes, as I did with Apple, you must let stocks go. Only in hindsight do the right decisions appear obvious, so go easy on yourself. This stuff is harder than it looks.

Postscript: The Apple example highlights the complexities of the sell decision, which I find far harder than any other. 'Why breaking up is hard to do' in the Appendix covers techniques to help improve your sell decisions.

Key takeaways from the stocks we sold too soon

While buying well and doing nothing is of tremendous value, there are very few businesses worthy of such loyalty. When you do happen to own them, hanging on is usually the best policy. When you fail to do so, it is most likely because you have become too anchored on price and value and been overconfident in your ability to assess the latter. High-quality businesses with the potential to compound over many years have a knack of providing positive surprises.

After not making the decision to sell, buying high-quality companies is the next most important call. This is best done when good stocks are going through bad times. Be aware that you will probably only recognise the opportunity once you have deeply researched the business, remembering that numbers alone are not enough, market share is not a guide to profitability, some companies are rule breakers and, as we learned with Star, politics doesn't matter until it really, really does.

When you own a high-compounding business, the preferable holding period is forever. This keeps your trading costs down and increases the effects of compounding by delaying tax. High portfolio turnover usually leads to poor performance. Reducing tax and trading costs and keeping portfolio turnover low improves performance.

Part III
Stocks We Should Not Have Bought at All

J ohn DeLorean thought he was onto a winner. During his General Motors (GM) career, he managed the development of the Pontiac GTO, named after the famous Ferrari 250 GTO, taking the brand to third place in annual US sales.[1] Other engineering and design successes followed, leading to his appointment in 1969 as head of GM's prestigious Chevrolet division. In his mid-forties, DeLorean was earning a salary equivalent to $2.5 million in 2024 dollars, with a bonus of up to $5 million.[2]

With open shirts and a maverick style, DeLorean's burgeoning reputation made him a celebrity. Then, he became friends with Sammy Davis Jr and *The Tonight Show* host Johnny Carson. Inviting Ford president Lee Iacocca to be best man at one of his four weddings was one of the many ways he got under the skin of his GM colleagues.

Still, no one knows whether DeLorean was sacked or resigned, but it didn't matter. DeLorean was a man destined to do things his way.

In 1973, set on building a futuristic two-seater sports car, the DeLorean Motor Company was founded. Thanks to a £100 million incentive from a government agency, the factory was established in Belfast, Northern Ireland. The car is best known for its role as the time-travelling vehicle driven by Michael J Fox's character Marty McFly in the *Back to the Future* movie trilogy.

The car was less successful than the movie in which it featured. By early 1982, just 7,000 DeLorean vehicles had been built, and half remained unsold.[3] Carrying US$175 million in debt, the factory was placed in receivership.[4] A few years later, after the UK government found monies extended to DeLorean had been transferred to Panama

---

1   en.wikipedia.org/wiki/Pontiac_GTO
2   en.wikipedia.org/wiki/John_DeLorean
3   en.wikipedia.org/wiki/John_DeLorean
4   deloreandirectory.com/reposts/receivership-declared-at-delorean/

and the US government had charged him with cocaine trafficking, the company entered liquidation.[5]

DeLorean beat the drug trafficking charges and further accusations of fraud, but he never recovered. He found that building cars in a place with no history of doing so was harder than being in Detroit and running a division of the biggest automobile company in the world.

Overconfident and under-skilled, DeLorean got the business model wrong. The car wasn't as innovative as it looked, it guzzled gas, and it cost too much to build. The company ran out of money just as the first car rolled off the production line, making sales paramount. The model was rushed to market with production faults, each one widely reported in the media. The DeLorean was dead on arrival, and its founder lost a fortune and his reputation.

The disasters recounted in this section feel bearable in comparison. We may have lost members substantial sums, but we survived. The lessons learned and the transparency displayed probably burnished our reputation rather than damaged it. As for the drugs charges, I make no comment.

Nevertheless, failures hurt. It is one thing to lose money on a stock by selling too early or too late. It is another to do so with a company you later realise you should never have bought at all. This is a categorically different kind of error. Getting the business model wrong, as did DeLorean, warrants a particular kind of introspection, so grab the popcorn, take a seat in the *Intelligent Investor* time machine and watch the horrors unfold.

---

5   history.com/this-day-in-history/john-z-delorean-is-arrested-in-24-million-cocaine-deal

Case Study #7
Timbercorp

The buy from hell, via the ATO

Between April 2007 and September 2008, we made 16 recommendations on Timbercorp – seven 'buys' and nine 'strong buys'. It went on to lose members up to 96 percent of their stake, making it our worst call ever. The problems began right from the very start.

What happened

The finance industry is hardwired for complexity. This isn't for performance reasons. There is no evidence that a complex financial strategy is more successful than something simple and easily understood. There is, however, a powerful financial reason to create convoluted, intricate products that don't work.

In the early 1990s, I ventured into the North Sydney offices of a financial planner. I had saved $5,000 and was looking for something to do with it. Big mistake. I explained my circumstances, and at our second meeting he outlined his recommendations. The product I forget; the cost I recall: a 4 percent entry fee and a one-off 5 percent set-up fee.

I was young and gullible. I didn't understand the big impact of small percentages on average returns and was too embarrassed to ask.

From his perspective, things were going to plan. The fees rationalised my confusion: these people must be geniuses. The sales approach was seasoned and deliberate, fashioned during the heyday of financial planning when people with little knowledge of compounding or percentages got screwed. Three years later, I found out how badly.

'Simplicity is a great virtue,' Dutch computer scientist Edsger Dijkstra once noted, 'but it requires hard work to achieve it and education to appreciate it. And to make matters worse: complexity sells better.'[1] In an avaricious industry, a bigger fee for less work or a lower fee for more is a simple choice. High fees, justified by complexity, win every time.

Whether my North Sydney planner sold Timbercorp products, I have no idea. Given the 10 percent commission Timbercorp paid financial advisers to promote their products, I'm sure he would have been tempted. For us, it should have been a warning sign. Instead, the implications of a fat fee were subsumed into our own complexity vortex.

What followed was a failure of monumental proportions (see Figure 6).

Figure 6: A long decline

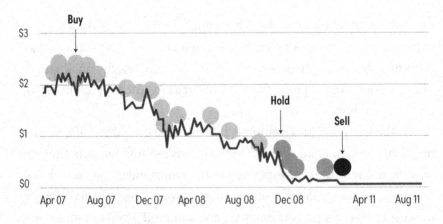

SOURCE: S&P CAPITAL IQ; *INTELLIGENT INVESTOR*

---

1   goodreads.com/quotes/215637-simplicity-is-a-great-virtue-but-it-requires-hard-work

Our first review of Timbercorp laid out the investment case. Asset booms and low unemployment had left many 'investors with a tax problem' – a euphemism for those who had made a lot of money but would prefer not to pay full freight on the tax. Timbercorp offered a solution in the form of managed investment schemes (MIS): it would purchase land, divide it into notional quarter-hectare blocks and plant a crop – timber, olives, mangoes, almonds or avocados. Investors would supply the financing, lured by the ability to claim 100 percent of the investment as an upfront tax deduction.

The pitch was so attractive it spawned an entire industry. By 2007, Federal Minister for Revenue Peter Dutton had wised up. Over $1 billion a year was being claimed in MIS-related deductions[2], and Dutton wanted to curtail it. From July 2008, investors in horticulture schemes were excluded from claiming upfront deductions, although timber-related schemes were still permissible.[3]

This was bad news for Timbercorp. In 2006, horticulture accounted for almost three-quarters of its revenue. Dutton's pen halved its share price. This, we thought, was the genesis of the opportunity. The company had locked-in future revenue increases from past sales that would almost offset the loss of income elsewhere. Trading on a price earnings ratio (PER) of less than seven, we plunged in.

A string of 'buy' recommendations followed, matched only by the regularity of dispiriting announcements from the company. The global financial crisis (GFC) and drought in its primary growing areas were hammer blows. With confidence in management ailing, we downgraded to 'hold' in late 2008 and eventually sold out for a total loss of 96 percent in April 2009. Six days later, the administrators were called in.

2   moneymanagement.com.au/features/editorial/danger-managed-investment-schemes
3   austlii.edu.au/au/journals/LegIssBus/2007/8.pdf

Why it happened

There were four reasons why Timbercorp became our worst invest-ment ever.

1. Business model misunderstanding

Ostensibly, Timbercorp sold timber and horticulture investments. Documentation promoting its schemes featured images of its plantations – rows of trees as far as the eye could see showing olives ripening in the sun. But what the company really sold were tax deductions.

Its existence depended on the government not doing something sensible, which would be to close the tax loopholes being exploited en masse. When Dutton moved to do so, the fragility of the company's business model was exposed. We underestimated this risk.

2. Over-reliance on debt

Timbercorp's business model was precariously funded. MIS schemes typically ran for 30 years but were financed with short-term debt. The balance sheet from 30 September 2006 showed net debt of $193 million. A year later it had more than doubled. Timbercorp's projects came with a fat 'capex tail' that required funding.

When the GFC hit, the appetite for debt increased and supply vanished. We underestimated the capital-intensive nature of the business. The effective closing of credit markets during the GFC crushed the company, taking any hope of recovery in its share price with it.

3. Prior success primed us for failure

Underestimating the company's exposure to debt and misreading its business model might not have happened had we not had previous success in the sector. Prior to Timbercorp, we almost tripled our money in two years on Forest Enterprises and made four times our original investment in a year on Great Southern Plantations.

During Timbercorp's slide from over $2 a share towards zero, there were warning signs, not just of a dud business but of poor management struggling with a deteriorating situation. There was evidence we might have gotten this one wrong, but we chose to ignore it. Our successful past experiences entrenched a belief that MIS companies were inherently stronger than they really were. Having made out like bandits on two companies, we downplayed the risks with another.

4. We were snared by commitment bias

When Timbercorp's 2007 half-year balance sheet was released a few months after our original 'strong buy' recommendation, we noted that most of the company's cash had disappeared. At that point, we realised this was a riskier proposition, but we neglected to sell.

That old favourite – commitment bias – explains why. Strong buys were rare. When they came along, many members acted on them. That made it hard for us to cut our losses. Having repeatedly issued our strongest recommendation, we felt subconscious pressure to remain consistent. This made it harder to accept the evidence that things were not playing out as we had hoped.

Lessons

Here are the lessons we learned from investing in Timbercorp.

1. Understand the business model

Many companies are not what they seem. Google appears to sell ads; what it really sells is data. BMW is a car manufacturer, but the brand markets status. And while Apple sells electronic gadgets such as iPhones, iPads and watches, what the purchaser pays for is an ecosystem built on convenience. As an investor, understanding the motivations of the purchaser is as important as comprehending the product.

Timbercorp looked like an agriculture company; what it really sold were tax deductions. Unlike cars, data or electronic devices, tax deductions exist courtesy of tax officials and politicians. And their favour can be easily revoked.

This is a risk that salary-packaging companies such as McMillan Shakespeare and Smartgroup face. In fact, any company that relies on a quirk of legislation has a precarious business model, and the MIS business model was precarious from the start.

2. Beware complexity

Risk is embedded in complexity. You are more likely to find fraud within a complex business than a simple one. I'd go even further: complexity itself is not only a risk but a warning sign.

Timbercorp was complex in many ways. It offered financially engineered products like those pitched to me by my financial planner. Complexity was a feature, not a bug; it was a means of justifying the outrageous fees.

The company was also subject to strict regulatory criteria that could be altered on a whim and had no direct contact with customers. Agriculture is also complicated, with large swings in input costs and weather. These factors added complexity to the business and the investment case. The best businesses to invest in are difficult to copy but easy to understand. Timbercorp was easy to copy and difficult to understand.

3. Excessive fees and commissions are a red flag

What does it say about a business that it needs to pay commissions to financial advisers to get a sale? This is not how good companies work; the quality of the product and its appreciation by customers should be enough. Tesla famously avoided intermediary salespeople and advertising for this reason. The high fees and commissions exposed by The Royal Commission into Misconduct in the Banking, Superannuation and Financial Services Industry were required because the products couldn't sell themselves. Advisers had to be bribed into selling something their clients didn't need and wouldn't benefit from.

When commissions account for a large slice of the margin on a sale, it's usually a problem. Buy companies for whom commissions are unnecessary because customers love their products. These tend to make better investments.

4. Mistakes are inevitable

Previously unforeseeable events – a change in regulation, unsustainable debt, a financial crisis – take on a degree of inevitability with time. Had Timbercorp worked out, the risks would not have changed. The outcome, however, would have meant you wouldn't be reading about it here. It didn't, and now, with hindsight, it seems obvious that it wouldn't.

This, too, is a trap. As behavioural psychologist Amos Tversky wrote: 'All too often, we find ourselves unable to predict what will happen; yet after the fact we explain what did happen with a great deal of confidence.'[4] The world is uncertain, and mistakes are inevitable. Once we accept that failure is integral to the process of being successful, wipe-outs like Timbercorp become easier to process.

Aftermath

Due to the scarcity of 'strong buys' and our repeated reiteration of that recommendation in the case of Timbercorp, some members allocated up to 30 percent of their portfolio to it. This was way more than advisable and provoked a change in *Intelligent Investor* policy. Since then, every recommendation has come with a suggested maximum portfolio limit.

Risk isn't just about whether you buy a stock or not, but also how much you allocate to it. Sensible portfolio allocation is central to

---

4   Michael Lewis, *The Undoing Project*, W.W. Norton, 2016.

successful investing. Companies with weak business models or poor management, or those in their early stages of growth, warrant a lower portfolio allocation than established, high-quality businesses.

We also now recommend that the average portfolio should not have more than 10 percent allocated to speculative stocks, with no single position accounting for more than 3 percent. This is what sensible portfolio management entails. There are cases where these rules should be broken, but only by confident, experienced investors. To avoid your very own Timbercorp, maintain sensible portfolio weightings. Don't put too much in a just a handful of stocks.

REFERENCES

- 10 Apr 2007: Timbercorp ripe for the picking (intelligentinvestor.com.au/recommendations/timbercorp-ripe-for-picking/55765)

- 18 May 2007: Profits axed at Timbercorp (intelligentinvestor.com.au/recommendations/profits-axed-at-timbercorp/55837)

- 10 Jan 2008: Timbercorp's debt worries (intelligentinvestor.com.au/recommendations/timbercorpand039s-debt-worries/56179)

- 16 May 2008: Bad debts top profit (intelligentinvestor.com.au/recommendations/bad-debts-lop-timbercorps-profit/56400)

- 13 Nov 2008: Worried about Timbercorp (intelligentinvestor.com.au/recommendations/worried-about-timbercorp/56717)

- 28 Nov 2008: T for trouble (intelligentinvestor.com.au/recommendations/t-for-trouble-at-timbercorp/56734)

- 9 Mar 2008: Shareholders get tough (intelligentinvestor.com.au/recommendations/shareholders-get-tough-on-timbercorp/56854)

- 17 Apr 2009: Timbercorp's darkest hour (intelligentinvestor.com.au/recommendations/timbercorpand039s-darkest-hour/56906)

- 23 Apr 2009: In administration (intelligentinvestor.com.au/investment-news/timbercorp-in-administration-select-harvests-in-trading-halt/56918)

Case Study #8
PMP

Gutenberg's value trap

PMP was an apparently cheap business operating in a difficult industry with a plan to improve it. The plan didn't work, and we sold out for a 64 percent loss. When competent managers fight a poor industry, it is the industry that usually wins.

What happened

In his 2007 Berkshire Hathaway shareholder letter, Warren Buffett wrote of the Wright brothers' invention of the aeroplane, 'If a far-sighted capitalist had been present at Kitty Hawk, he would have done his successors a huge favor by shooting Orville down.'[1] Armed with another bullet, said capitalist might have also taken out Johannes Gutenberg. No technology has advanced humanity as much as the printing press; compared to the printed word, even the miracle of flight is a sideshow. For investors, however, both have been disasters.

As in aviation, expensive new technologies consign old ones to the scrapheap. Printers know this all too well, which is why they are either

---

1   berkshirehathaway.com/letters/2007ltr.pdf

excited about their new presses or worried about their competitors' latest purchase. A new printing press will offer an advantage, but only until the rest of the industry catches up. Meanwhile, the pressure is on everyone to keep the work flowing. An idle machine, like an aircraft untroubled by passengers, is a quick way to go broke.

This leads the industry to a dark place: printers compete not to make a profit but merely to stay alive. Ensuring their machines are permanently occupied, working on paper-thin margins, is how they do it. These are the bread-and-butter facts of a terrible industry. The best chance of making money in it is to be the last one standing.

That was our aim when we first called PMP a 'speculative buy' in mid-2015. Its financial performance reflected the industry's awful economics. Profit margins had been negative in five of the previous six years, revenues had declined for a decade, returns on capital were woeful and industry conditions diabolical. In other words, business as usual. Between 1995 and 2015, PMP's share price had fallen 80 percent.

More recent evidence pointed to a possible turnaround. Debt had been paid down, costs had been slashed and the asset base had been restructured. There was even the possibility of dividends. A new business model beckoned, and investors were seduced by the possibility. In the three years prior to our initial purchase, PMP's share price had risen 260 percent.

The printed catalogues that clogged the nation's letterboxes were the fatbergs of the marketing sewerage system. But they worked. In 2015, catalogues reached more people each week than free-to-air TV, radio and newspapers.[2] For retailers such as JB Hi-Fi, the supermarkets and Harvey Norman, catalogues were an extremely cost-effective marketing channel.

Having spent $200 million over the previous five years, mainly on new printing machines, PMP's plan was to lock in the big retail chains

---

2   bandt.com.au/marketers-underestimating-catalogue-power/

at attractive rates and push higher-cost operators out of the industry, or acquire them at knockdown prices.

The subsequent consolidation, we calculated, should allow profit margins to increase from 2 to 3 percent. This seemingly small increase would have a big impact. PMP's earnings could rise by a third. Were that to occur, PMP looked incredibly cheap.

The company's aim was to become a key player – the last person standing, in effect, in a niche market. At a price of 53 cents, like Orville Wright at Kitty Hawk, we climbed aboard and strapped ourselves in. PMP joined the buy list as a speculative purchase with a maximum portfolio weighting of 3 percent.

The Wright Flyer travelled barely 100 feet on its first flight, but at least it got airborne. PMP never left the ground. Three years later, recognising a loss of 64 percent, we sold out.

Why it happened

There were three basic reasons why we got PMP wrong.

1. We backed the wrong horse

The printing industry suffered from excess capacity. We believed PMP's high free cash flows could be used to purchase competitors, producing a newly rationalised industry with higher margins. This is what happened. PMP and listed competitor IVE Group turned five competitors into two.

Their fortunes then diverged. After acquiring two competitors, IVE doubled margins. PMP's purchase of the number two player IPMG didn't go as well. After the merger, PMP *lowered* profit forecasts to half what was expected when the merger was announced. Capacity was cut, utilisation rose and industry conditions improved, but it was PMP's key competitor, IVE, that reaped the rewards. We got the race right but backed the wrong horse.

2. Consolidation didn't lead to better industry economics

Investors regularly buy into companies on the basis that consolidation will improve industry economics. IVE played their part in that dynamic, but margins didn't improve enough. The major players couldn't kick their competitive mindset and addiction to new printers. A positive change in industry economics required a change in culture, and that failed to materialise.

3. Irrational competition followed rationalisation

Stock analysts and market commentators love a euphemism. 'Rational competition', a phrase for when a small number of dominant companies tacitly agree not to compete on price, is an example. We believed catalogue printing, with just two major players, would become an example of the kind of 'rational' competition on display among airlines, banks and supermarkets – neither too hot nor too cold, but just right.

That didn't happen, either. At the time of our first sell recommendation, PMP announced it was 'investing' another $20 million on a whizzbang new printer. The previous capex binge had led management to disavow any new investment for years. Despite the new market structure, the habit could not be kicked. Customers, via lower prices, won at the expense of shareholders. The industry structure had changed; the mentality that predated it hadn't.

Lessons

Here are the lessons we learned from investing in PMP.

1. Poor industries usually make terrible investments

In mediocre industries – a misleadingly benevolent adjective for printing – the chances of things not working out are higher than they are in more profitable, less cutthroat sectors. This is true regardless of management competence, industry size and product quality.

No matter how cheap a low-quality business looks, it is probably not cheap enough for the risks you'll bear. Poor businesses tend to stay poor. PMP was a poor business in a challenging sector. Its financial performance all the way through proved it. We should have avoided the sector altogether.

2. Patience is good; stubbornness is not

We waited three years before deciding PMP wasn't going to work out. With the benefit of hindsight, the evidence came after two years, when a devastating profit downgrade slashed the share price by 30 percent. We wanted to be patient because we knew that was our edge. In retrospect, we were stubborn rather than patient. Inflexibility stopped us from seeing what we didn't want to know. A value investor's instinct for forbearance and grit worked against us.

3. The simple ideas are the best

Making money from a poor business is possible, but it will demand much of your time and all your investigative expertise. It will also require a suite of psychological skills that most investors lack. Even with these attributes, your odds of making money from a poor business aren't great.

It is easier and usually better to stick to investing in good companies in growing sectors, where things are more likely to go for rather than against you. Don't be seduced by complexity, an apparently cheap price and the notion that you are smarter than everyone else. The simple ideas are the best.

Aftermath

After combining with IPMG in 2017, PMP became known as Ovato.[3] The name change didn't cover the cracks. Job losses mounted and printing contracts were lost. In the year to July 2022, Ovato's share price

---

3   thewire.fiig.com.au/article/2016/11/08/pmp-to-acquire-ipmg

fell almost 70 percent. Towards the end of that month, the company collapsed. In September 2022, IVE confirmed it had acquired most of Ovato's assets.[4] The price paid was just $16 million. IVE, not PMP, had become the last person standing.

And yet the consolidation we forecast still didn't produce the returns we expected. IVE's revenue increased substantially through its acquisitions and net profit margins did indeed increase, from 2 percent in 2021 to 4.6 percent in 2023, but over the same three years, cash on the balance sheet more than halved and net gearing increased.

A more-or-less flat share price over eight years reflects the difficulty. IVE's management proved more capable than PMP's, but the poor quality of the industry prevailed. Since it became the last person standing, IVE has delivered slightly worse than market returns.

PMP was a 'value trap', a company that appeared to trade cheaply but which faced challenging conditions that more than offset its apparently cheap price. IVE wasn't much better. To fall into a value trap is to misidentify value. The market had PMP right; we got it wrong.

PMP inadvertently makes the case for buying high-quality businesses at reasonable prices rather than poor businesses at cheap prices. Terrible managers find it hard to destroy a good business, while excellent managers find it tough to eke out modest returns from a bad one. A good business with excellent management, acquired at a reasonable price, is where you'll find your biggest winners. An apparently cheap business in an ailing industry is where you will make your biggest losses.

REFERENCES

· 19 Jun 2015: PMP back from the brink (intelligentinvestor.com.au/recommendations/pmp-back-from-the-brink/61081)

· 23 Nov 2015: Pressing on (intelligentinvestor.com.au/recommendations/pmp-pressing-on/61388)

---

4   sprinter.com.au/ive-completes-16m-acquisition-of-parts-of-ovato/

- 6 Jan 2016: Dick Smith bust bites PMP (intelligentinvestor.com.au/recommendations/dick-smith-bust-bites-pmp/61482)
- 28 Oct 2016: Patience pays (intelligentinvestor.com.au/recommendations/patience-pays-at-pmp/138388)
- 17 Feb 2017: PMP merger gets green light (intelligentinvestor.com.au/recommendations/pmp-merger-gets-green-light/138915)
- 9 Jun 2017: The new duopolist (intelligentinvestor.com.au/recommendations/pmp-the-new-duopolist/139461)
- 21 Nov 2017: When cracks appear (intelligentinvestor.com.au/recommendations/pmp-when-cracks-appear/141833)
- 14 Feb 2018: Profit warning (intelligentinvestor.com.au/recommendations/pmp-profit-warning/142188)
- 7 Mar 2018: Merger blues (intelligentinvestor.com.au/recommendations/pmps-merger-blues/142315)
- 5 Sep 2018: Repair and despair (intelligentinvestor.com.au/recommendations/pmp-repair-and-despair/143147)

Case Study #9
Amaysim

Downwardly mobile

In a corner of the mobile market, Amaysim was so dominant even its main supplier relied upon it for new customers. Then came a vicious price war from which the company never recovered. This is the story of how competition killed Amaysim, producing a staggering loss.

What happened

Between the frozen foods and household goods aisles at Woolworths, Port Melbourne, is a seemingly endless row of laundry powders and a bewildering array of brands. The choice is deceptive. Just two multinational corporations control most of the Australian laundry powder market: US-based Procter & Gamble owns brands like Tide, Ariel and Bold, while Anglo-Dutch Unilever owns Surf, OMO and Persil. What appears an ultra-competitive market is an illusion concealed by the prevalence of multiple brands owned by two companies.

Australia's mobile market is similar. In the way that P&G and Unilever dominate laundry powder, Telstra and Optus dominate mobile network access (Vodafone – remember them? – is a long third). Telstra accounts for 43 percent of the mobile market, Optus 29 percent and Vodafone 17 percent.[1]

The remainder is serviced by resellers known as 'mobile virtual network operators' (MVNOs). This is where the mobile sector diverges from a laundry-like cosy duopoly. MVNOs operate in a cutthroat sector that can instantly upend a stock recommendation. In the case of Amaysim, the upending resulted in a 53 percent loss.

At the time of our initial buy recommendation in March 2016, Amaysim had a contract with Optus to lease a slice of its 3G and 4G mobile networks at wholesale rates. It then marketed plans devised for retail customers. Optus provided the network; Amaysim took care of the marketing, billing, top-ups and customer service.

The MVNO model is used worldwide and has led to genuine competition. The major carriers suck up most of the sector's revenue, but MVNOs keep them honest. The majors like the revenue, too. Freed from the expense of acquiring and servicing customers, Amaysim's arrangement offered Optus the prospect of reliable, high-margin revenue just from selling capacity that would otherwise go unused.

Establishing and maintaining a mobile network is capital-intensive. As with airlines and electricity networks, higher usage leads to higher margins. By targeting market niches avoided by Optus and Telstra, MVNOs can increase the profitability of network operators through increased volume, offering the majors steady revenue. They also give themselves a shot at the big time if things work out.

By 2016, Amaysim had added 800,000 customers to the Optus network, and the big time beckoned. Our investment case was built on it acquiring many more users and growing average revenue per user (ARPU). On a price earnings ratio (PER) of over 40, we were confident it would do so.

There were three prongs to the investment case. First, Amaysim had operational leverage. Its largest cost was the network charge paid to Optus, equivalent to around 65 percent of revenue. This meant that

1   statista.com/statistics/488511/australia-mobile-handset-services-market-share/

as customer numbers grew, so did payments to Optus. Other costs, such as billing, marketing, service and activation, were largely fixed.

This is known as 'operating leverage'. As Amaysim acquired more customers, unit costs should theoretically fall, meaning revenue should grow faster than costs. The company's results at the time supported this proposition. Amaysim had first turned a profit with 600,000 customers. Once it reached 1 million customers, we calculated it would become extremely profitable, more than justifying its high PER.

The company's second advantage was its lower cost base. At the time, Optus had two SIM-only plans, five prepaid plans and five postpaid plans, each with multiple handset options. Like the laundry aisle at a local supermarket, complexity and confusion was part of the business model. Amaysim offered four plans and no handsets, instantly removing significant costs imposed by multiple products and handset subsidies. It also had fewer employees than Optus and, as most of its business was conducted online, no stores.

Here was a fast-growing company with an ultra-competitive cost base. Also, because Optus paid an upfront fee to Amaysim for each customer added to its network, to be paid back over two years, Optus effectively funded Amaysim's growth interest-free.

The third prong concerned the company's size. MVNOs were vital to Optus. Without them, Optus's user base would have been stagnant. That made Amaysim's negotiating position stronger than it appeared. Optus needed Amaysim's customers as much as Amaysim needed Optus's network.

The network supply agreement between Amaysim and Optus could be cancelled or renegotiated. This was a risk. If Optus ended the arrangement, Amaysim would need to strike a deal with another network operator and send all its customers replacement SIM cards. However, given the importance of the arrangement to Optus, this was as unpalatable and costly as it was unlikely.

In March 2016, at a price of $1.90, Amaysim became a 'speculative buy' with a maximum portfolio weighting of 3 percent and a business risk and share price risk rating of 'high'. Subsequent events proved every part of that sentence correct except for the word 'buy'. Just over two years later, we sold out, recognising a 53 percent loss.

Why it happened

There were three reasons why our investment in Amaysim turned bad.

1. Vicious price competition

For a year or so, the investment case played out as expected. Between 2015 and 2017, earnings before interest, tax, depreciation and amortisation (EBITDA) margins doubled as Amaysim's subscribers grew and operating leverage kicked in. Then, competition intensified, leading to falling ARPU. Customer numbers weren't rising fast enough to avoid a sharp fall in profits. Competition from the likes of Kogan and other MVNOs had reversed operating leverage.

Then, in 2018, TPG's entry into the mobile market smashed the investment case to smithereens. TPG founder David Teoh, a notorious cost-cutter, had determined to set the mobile market on its head. It was common knowledge that TPG was building a mobile network; what was less well known was its industry-upending pricing structure. TPG offered six months of 4G network access with unlimited data for free, after which it charged $10 a month. Amaysim's $10 plan offered just one gigabyte of data per month. As for Telstra, it was luxuriating in an ARPU of $65 per month. TPG's mobile pricing was the most aggressive the sector had seen. It killed the Amaysim investment case.

2. Amaysim changed strategy

Amaysim had set out to dominate the MVNO sector. In terms of customers, if not profitability, it had largely succeeded. Competition had intensified, however, and margins were falling. Amaysim responded with lower prices and a change in direction.

In April 2017, it purchased Click Energy, an electricity reseller. Electricity, like mobile services, is capital-intensive. With overlapping business models, Amaysim thought it a good fit. The ultimate objective was to market three products – mobile, NBN and electricity – on a single platform.

It seemed a sensible plan. The cross-sell model was common in Europe and, if Click grew at the expected rate, the money paid for it could be justified. With a long and growing list of customers, and an operating model that enshrined low customer acquisition costs and low operating costs, we stuck with it. That was a mistake.

3. Operating leverage went into reverse

Amaysim had to lower prices to compete with TPG. An impressive performance from the fast-growing energy business was not enough to arrest the decline in mobiles, nor was the fact that Optus appeared to have absorbed a large chunk of the lower ARPU burden.

As lower-priced plans and higher data inclusions spread, ARPU continued falling and profitability declined rapidly. The original argument for buying the company – operating leverage – had gone into reverse.

Lessons

Here are the lessons we learned from investing in Amaysim.

1. Always examine a company's competitive environment

While most of Australia's major industries are cosy duopolies, the MVNO sector is an example of how capitalism should work. Amaysim's industry position looked impregnable. Then TPG wiped it out, providing customers with network access and data at previously unimaginable prices. The competition was great for customers but terrible for Amaysim shareholders.

Everything in investing is contingent. The competitive environment in which a company operates is perhaps the biggest swing factor, which is why we deemed Amaysim's business risk 'high'. There is a tendency to focus on a company and its performance at the expense of its competitive environment, and yet this kind of examination will tell you how resistant a business model is to disruption. Do not neglect it.

2. When the model changes, so does the investment case

Amaysim's purchase of Click Energy was presented as a diversification. Internationally, many MVNOs used mobile markets to jump into the reselling of energy and broadband. This legitimised Amaysim's expansion, and the financials substantiated it. In the first half of the 2018 financial year, the company's energy operations generated more revenue and almost as much underlying profit as mobile.

But that is not why we bought the stock. We had purchased a mobile disruptor with a better business model than its competitors. By the time of the Click acquisition, we owned a mobile disrupter with an ailing model that needed rescuing. The investment case had changed, and we stuck with it, only for TPG to wield the final blow.

Whenever a company moves in an unexpected direction, exiting is usually the best course of action. Amaysim might have made the energy business work, and its strategy to sell three services rather than one made sense. But that was not why we originally purchased it. The acquisition tore up the roadmap. A change in the business model changes the investment case. When this occurs, re-examine your position with an eye towards getting out.

3. High-quality businesses have competitive defences

Our experience with Amaysim demonstrates the difference between low- and high-quality businesses. Amaysim wasn't a bad business when we purchased it, but it wasn't great either. The MVNO market was highly competitive. We thought Amaysim's competitive advantage was its size and its skill at acquiring customers.

Our faith proved misplaced. The data plans Amaysim sold had become a commodity. Commodity markets are typified by price competition, so businesses in these markets tend to make for poor investments. It is better to seek out businesses with competitive advantages that relate to factors other than price.

4. Weak competitive position is a signal to avoid

The MVNO market had low barriers to entry and required little investment in infrastructure or skills. Anyone with an idea and the money to fund it could sell mobile phone network access. Amaysim might have done it better than anyone else, but that was not a competitive advantage.

This was a signal. Amaysim was doing well but lacked any sustainable features that gave it ballast against an aggressive competitor. In the lingua franca of investing, it lacked a 'moat'. It didn't have Telstra's network quality, Optus's financial firepower or TPG's ruthlessness and fibre network.

While it was good at acquiring customers, mobile was becoming a price-driven commodity market. Amaysim was a good competitor in an increasingly competitive space, but this is not the material from which successful investments are made. We should have avoided it altogether.

Aftermath

The mobile market is an example of the power and absence of competitive advantage. Telstra's mobile business generates the highest margins in the world[2], mainly because the competition is so feeble. Optus suffers regular technical failures, and Vodafone, now merged with TPG, is crippled by a subscale network.

Customers are willing to pay handsomely for Australia's most reliable and extensive network. In August 2023, the mobile business accounted for $605 million of Telstra's $606 million increase in operating profits.[3] Price is the last thing Telstra must compete on. It is likely to stay that way. To preserve its dominance, Telstra reinvests about 16 percent of group revenues into mobile infrastructure and

2   intelligentinvestor.com.au/recommendations/stop-trying-to-fix-telstra/153315
3   intelligentinvestor.com.au/recommendations/telstra-result-2023/152836

spectrum.[4] The company's other businesses are poor in comparison. Shareholders would be better off without them, although management appears unwilling to let them go.

The competitive dynamics in the adjacent field of broadband are different. The National Broadband Network (NBN) supplies broadband access, selling wholesale to anyone who wants it. The market is intensely competitive by design. Although it is now dominated by Telstra, Optus, Vocus and Aussie Broadband, returns are suitably mediocre.

Except, that is, for Aussie Broadband, which has excelled at attracting high-value customers willing to pay more for faster speeds. Almost half of its user base have plans that cost over $100 a month.[5] Its ARPU, at $80 a month, is one of the highest in the industry.[6] Exceptional customer service and owning its own fibre explain the margins its competitors fail to match. Aussie has become the broadband version of what we hoped Amaysim might have become for mobile.

TPG's assault on Amaysim became a sideshow in a bigger war fought by founder David Teoh. Vodafone operated Australia's third mobile network while TPG excelled in broadband, gaining a 25 percent market share. Teoh had committed TPG to build its own mobile network but changed tack, proposing a merger between the two companies.[7] Whilst the Australian Competition and Consumer Commission (ACCC) objected, in mid-2020 the deal went through. The new company became known as TPG Telecom, chaired by David Teoh. Then, in March 2021, he abruptly resigned.[8]

An important person's unexpected and immediate resignation is never a good sign. The Lowys selling out of Westfield and James Packer

4   intelligentinvestor.com.au/recommendations/stop-trying-to-fix-telstra/153315
5   intelligentinvestor.com.au/recommendations/aussie-broadband-result-2023/152888
6   intelligentinvestor.com.au/recommendations/aussie-broadbands-big-switch/151826
7   vodafone.com/news/technology-news/vodafone-group-announces-merger-between-vha-and-tpg
8   afr.com/companies/telecommunications/teoh-son-quit-tpg-board-20210326-p57e9g

offloading PBL were both prescient indicators. Having recommended TPG as a buy a few weeks earlier, we saw the red flag and acted, selling out few weeks after it had joined the buy list.

From the hurly-burly of the Strathfield era to MVNOs like Amaysim, the mobile market now looks more like the settled oligopolies common to Australian consumers. Perhaps the ACCC was right. Telstra, Optus and TPG Telecom now control almost 90 percent of the retail phone market and 95 percent of the postpaid market.[9] All three have consistently raised prices since the merger went through. Prior to it, then-Telstra CEO Andy Penn described the merger as a 'good thing'.[10] Now we know what he meant.

REFERENCES

- 23 Mar 2016: Unlocking value in Amaysim (intelligentinvestor.com.au/recommendations/unlocking-value-in-amaysim/61988)
- 23 August 2016: Result 2016 (intelligentinvestor.com.au/recommendations/amaysim-result-2016/136594)
- 28 Feb 2017: Interim result (intelligentinvestor.com.au/recommendations/amaysim-interim-result-2017/138979)
- 13 Apr 2017: Amaysim Clicks on power (intelligentinvestor.com.au/recommendations/amaysim-clicks-on-power/139197)
- 1 Sep 2017: Result 2017 (intelligentinvestor.com.au/recommendations/amaysim-result-2017/139881)
- 8 Feb 2018: Profit warning (intelligentinvestor.com.au/recommendations/amaysim-warns-on-profits/142126)
- 5 Mar 2018: Downwardly mobile (intelligentinvestor.com.au/recommendations/amaysim-downwardly-mobile/142307)
- 9 Apr 2018: The mobile price war is here (intelligentinvestor.com.au/recommendations/the-mobile-price-war-is-here/142445)
- 21 May 2018: TPG kills Amaysim model (intelligentinvestor.com.au/recommendations/tpg-kills-the-amaysim-model/142633)
- 24 Apr 2019: Rethinking Amaysim (intelligentinvestor.com.au/recommendations/rethinking-amaysim/144756)

Key takeaways from the stocks we should not have bought at all

Before buying a stock, ensure you understand its business model – how and why it makes money, or aims to do so – and its competitive environment. Competitive defences are signs of high-quality businesses, which usually make for good investments. Businesses in poor industries usually do not. Excessive fees and commissions are signs of a product that might otherwise be hard to sell. Vicious price competition is another signal of a crappy industry.

Beware complexity. The simple ideas are the best. Watch out for radical changes in strategy. When you spot them, revisit the original investment case. Patience is good; stubbornness is not.

Don't expect rationality – in industries, companies or your own decision-making. Prior success primes us for future failure, and the commitment principle means mistakes are inevitable. Your purpose, like the aim of this book, is to make better mistakes rather than none at all.

Part IV
Stocks We Should Have Bought but Didn't

B uried in a rubbish dump in Newport, south Wales, is a hard drive containing 8,000 Bitcoin units. At least, that is what its former owner, systems engineer James Howells, believes.[1] Assuming the data can be recovered – and Howells is convinced it can – the hard drive's current value is about $780 million. Howells has mounted a decade-long and thus far unsuccessful campaign to convince the local council to let him search for it.

Met with repeated denials, he has resorted to enlightened bribery, promising to donate a quarter of the funds rescued to the local community should he gain access and retrieve the disk. This, too, has been rejected, but Howells has not given up. Until he relinquishes the thought of what might have been, he is unlikely to do so.

Everyone regrets the riches they let slip. Ours include Pro Medicus, a medical software company that listed in late 2000 at a price of $1.25. Sixteen years later, it was trading at around $5. During that period, we regularly admired its qualities but failed to act. In the last decade, it has risen to around $115.

We repeated the mistake with WiseTech Global, a logistics software business. It listed in April 2016 at a price of $3.35 and is now careering towards $100 a share. Like Pro Medicus and Xero, a thirty bagger we missed out on, it never troubled our buy list.

There are many more examples. None are featured in this section because, having examined these companies and admired their qualities, they were deemed too expensive. As with Cochlear, ARB and Apple, all stocks we sold too soon, we underestimated their intrinsic value, making the price appear more expensive than it was.

So far, this book has been about errors of commission – decisions that subsequently proved wrong. There is another category of

---

1   bbc.co.uk/news/uk-wales-67297013

mistake – failing to act when we should. This section concerns our lost hard drives, our mistakes of omission. And yet we do not regret them as might James Howells. Missing out on high-quality, seemingly expensive companies is in the nature of the endeavour.

Value investors like to buy companies for less than they think they are worth. The recipe for doing so is simple to explain but hard to do:

1. Buy companies that solve a genuine problem for their customers.
2. Gather evidence they can reinvest cash flows over decades to extend their competitive advantages.
3. Ensure the founders and managers have enough stock to behave like owners rather than seat warmers.
4. Purchase them at attractive prices with a margin of safety.
5. When it makes sense, hold them for decades.

This is how you find an eventual hundred bagger, a stock that rises 10,000 percent. You may be aware of some examples: CSL, REA Group (the owner of realestate.com.au) and Altium have all risen over 10,000 percent since listing. Spotting them is relatively easy. Paying a suitable price is the challenge. Great companies rarely trade cheaply, and when they do, there is usually some justification for it.

Investing is not a science. Assessing the value of a stock is loaded with assumptions and saddled with the biases of those making the calculations. There is an art to it, an imperfection that is both a fountain of error and a source of beauty. As time passes, the list of stocks that got away from you will lengthen. This is the cost of discipline. The benefit is in the stocks you don't overpay for.

Everything in life is a trade-off. In investing, the cost of reducing the risk of paying too much for a stock is the occasional rocket ship you fail to board. It is a price worth paying. You can't buy everything that goes up, nor should you aim to. As you shall see, there is great danger in trying.

Sometimes, you will find an impressive company and not get the chance to buy at a reasonable price. Occasionally, an opportunity arrives, and for some reason you fail to act. The case studies that follow aim to help you hit more than you miss. They're followed by some advice on the dangers of seeking out big winners like Afterpay, a hundred bagger we never wanted to buy despite the returns it delivered.

Case Study #10
Meta

Missing the fat pitch

An investing lifetime entails a mere handful of truly great opportunities. When one comes along, it is best to swing big. This is the story of Meta – of how I saw the ball coming, did all the work and failed to even pick up the bat, missing out on a 500 percent gain.

What happened

It had not been a great 12 months for Mark Zuckerberg.

In April 2021, Apple introduced App Tracking Transparency (ATT)[1], ostensibly in response to privacy concerns. Users were realising that sites like Facebook tracked them everywhere online; ATT rendered the tiny dot Facebook deployed to do so useless. Without the data firehose this tiny pixel delivered, the company's ability to finely target customers was at risk, exactly as Apple had planned. Advertisers were concerned.

So were politicians, albeit for different reasons. Evidence was mounting that social media was damaging mental health, particularly

---

1   techcrunch.com/2021/04/26/apples-app-tracking-transparency-feature-has-arrived-heres-what-you-need-to-know

among children. Critics claimed Facebook's apps played a role in online bullying and suicidal ideation. In October 2021, Frances Haugen, a former Facebook product manager, claimed before a US Senate sub-committee that the company prioritised profits over user safety.

'Here's my message for Mark Zuckerberg,' said committee member Senator Ed Markey in response. 'Your time of invading our privacy, promoting toxic content and preying on children and teens is over.'[2] As Haugen was giving testimony, Zuckerberg posted a video of himself and his wife Priscilla Chan on a giant yacht.[3]

Later that month, Facebook rebranded as Meta to reflect its focus on building the metaverse, although no one really knew what that was. Despite investing billions, the company's product to bring it about – the Meta Quest virtual reality headset – had mixed reviews and a user base that would fit into a cereal packet. The metaverse felt like a Zuckerberg fever dream.

TikTok, the short-form video platform, was also gaining traction. In 2021, it had grown by 40 percent, and its Stories product was threatening to engulf Instagram. Zuckerberg's response was to release a version of it targeted at children under the age of 13. The outrage was sufficient for the company to quickly pull it.[4]

Meta had become a public enemy and Zuckerberg was under attack. For some, he was killing democracy and childhood, a quinella even beyond the reach of Rupert Murdoch. Others thought him an amoral laughing-stock in a nerd helmet. Few had anything good to say about him or the company he founded, especially among the media.

The Guardian, effortlessly echoing the late Czech-French novelist Milan Kundera, wrote of 'Mark Zuckerberg's unbearable sadness.'[5]

---

2   nytimes.com/2021/10/05/technology/facebook-whistle-blower-hearing.html
3   cnbc.com/2021/10/05/congress-demands-mark-zuckerberg-answer-questions-at-haugen-hearing.html
4   about.instagram.com/blog/announcements/pausing-instagram-kids
5   theguardian.com/technology/2022/aug/31/techscape-facebook-meta-the-unbearable-sadness-of-mark-zuckerberg

Forbes revealed he upgraded his 'Metaverse' Avatar 'after the entire Internet laughed at him'.[6]

The Australian press joined the fun, *The Sydney Morning Herald* gloating that Zuckerberg had 'lost more than half his fortune in a year'.[7] *The Australian Financial Review*, perhaps self-referentially, called the Meta rebrand 'a colossal fail'.[8] Even in a country where wealth and defamation laws insulate the rich from criticism, Zuck had become his own meme, an out-of-touch caricature of a billionaire who thought everyone else was the problem.

Then, things got worse. In early September 2021, Meta's share price had hit an all-time high of around US$378. The adverse publicity, the political fury and a series of screw-ups then had their cumulative effect. In just over a year, the price collapsed to under US$100.

Meta was under attack from every quarter. In early November 2022, at almost US$90, the share price was at its lowest point in seven years. Meta was trading on a single-digit PER, priced as if it were about to suffer a slow death surrounded by gleeful onlookers.

Investors talk of the fat pitch, a baseball term in which the batter sees a ball so well they can hardly fail to knock it out of the park. Fat pitches are rare. In the last 25 years, I've had only a few. Each was a terrific opportunity, usually accompanied by a media pile-on.

Fat pitches tend to be great companies going through hard times. As the media amplifies the company's problems, the share price falls. The often very real risks are exaggerated.

There are risks with every investment, but with fat pitches they tend to be small in comparison to the opportunity. These life-changing investments can make you five or ten times your money. If there is a case for defying the rules of portfolio allocation and putting 10 or

6   forbes.com/sites/danidiplacido/2022/08/21/mark-zuckerberg-upgraded-his-metaverse-avatar-after-the-entire-internet-laughed-at-him

7   smh.com.au/business/companies/106b-wipeout-mark-zuckerberg-has-lost-more-than-half-his-fortune-in-a-year-20220920-p5bjds.html

8   afr.com/technology/zuckerberg-s-metaverse-looks-like-a-colossal-fail-20221017-p5bqaj

even 20 percent of your portfolio into a single company, at least for experienced investors, fat pitches are it.

At $90 a share in November 2022, Meta was the plumpest of fat pitches. And yet, despite spending months researching it and becoming convinced the fears were overdone, I failed to act. The ball was big, I saw it coming and I didn't even take a swing.

Why it happened

Late in 2022, Zuckerberg wrote to his employees 'sharing some of the most difficult changes we've made in Meta's history'.[9] That change was to lay off 11,000 people. The public took it as a sign of a desperate company in decline. In retrospect, it was the start of the turnaround.

There were four narratives that smashed Meta's share price. The first concerned Apple's ATT policy and its effect on advertising. This severed the link between Meta's advertising products and user activity on third-party (non-Meta) websites. Without such data, Meta's advertising became less valuable to clients – being less targeted meant it was less effective. Meta admitted as much: accompanying the company's results in early 2022 was commentary that ATT could reduce revenue by some US$10 billion a year.[10] Apple was going after Meta's core revenue, and Meta, the story went, was defenceless in the face of attack.

The second threat came from TikTok. Its rise corresponded with Instagram's lower growth rates. Investors concluded that TikTok was slowly eating its lunch.

The third was Facebook saturation. With almost 3 billion monthly active users[11], accompanied by the stench surrounding social media, decline seemed inevitable.

9   about.fb.com/news/2022/11/mark-zuckerberg-layoff-message-to-employees/
10 cnbc.com/2022/02/02/facebook-says-apple-ios-privacy-change-will-cost-10-billion-this-year.html
11 thesocialshepherd.com/blog/facebook-statistics

The fourth and final narrative decimating Meta's share price was Zuckerberg's costly pipedream. By late 2022, Meta had invested about US$36 billion in the metaverse since 2019[12], but it had little to show for it. Zuckerberg's public statements suggested his obsession would persist.

Meta was facing existential threats to its core advertising business and was losing market share to new competition. Worse, its proposed way out of the mess was a fairytale business strategy with an unhappy ending.

Over the Christmas holidays I read as much as I could about Meta and Tesla, which was being similarly lambasted. My conclusions differed from the popular narratives; neither survived scrutiny.

The metaverse project *was* expensive and perhaps futile, but history suggested Zuckerberg was sufficiently pragmatic to cut spending if needed. Laying off 13 percent of his workforce in November 2022 suggested so. Even if he wasn't, Meta was still hugely profitable. If any company could afford to lose US$10 billion a year on a blinkered long shot, this was it.

Whilst Facebook was reaching saturation, it was still growing, mainly in the less profitable Asia-Pacific region. But user numbers in the more profitable markets of Europe and North America were flat rather than declining. Even if decline set in, it would take decades for Facebook to slip into irrelevance and loss. Believe it or not, Myspace is still going and in 2023 Friendster was revived, although it could be a phishing scam.[13] The hatred directed at social media does not stop people from using it.

The threat from TikTok was more serious. Recognising the challenge, Meta had acted early, introducing Reels to Instagram and Facebook in mid-2020.[14] This was more evidence of Meta's willingness to shamelessly copy features from other applications.

---

12 businessinsider.com/meta-lost-30-billion-on-metaverse-rivals-spent-far-less-2022-10
13 malwarebytes.com/blog/news/2022/12/friendster-is-back-or-is-it
14 about.instagram.com/blog/announcements/introducing-instagram-reels-announcement

In 2016, Instagram had introduced Stories to compete with the popular Snapchat.[15] Within two years, it had twice as many daily users.[16] More recently, Meta took advantage of Elon Musk's Twitter woes to launch Threads.[17] Zuckerberg has a history of responding to competitive threats and prevailing.

Meta also had the advantage of incumbency. Its ad products were more developed than TikTok's, while its American rather than Chinese ownership was another positive. Short-form video advertising may have been growing, and TikTok was grabbing its share, but it was not eating into Meta's revenue, only reducing its rate of growth. And, as with Snapchat and Reels, the company was responding to the threat.

Apple's introduction of ATT was the biggest and most justifiable concern. The digital advertising market was growing quickly, and Facebook retained a huge and unmatched data trove acquired before its introduction. Meta was the go-to advertising channel for new start-ups, and Zuckerberg was diverting funds from his pet project to artificial intelligence to reduce ATT's impact. There were early signs Meta would be successful at combatting the threat.[18]

Slowly, these factors began to challenge the doomy narrative. In early 2023, Meta's share price started to rise. By the time of its quarterly results in early 2024, it was up fivefold. More remarkable were the financial results driving it.

In the previous few years, Meta had reduced its workforce by a quarter, supposedly in a desperate attempt to cut costs and stave off decline. The company's February 2024 quarterly numbers showed how wrong this narrative had been. Revenue had increased by 25 percent.[19] The TikTok threat had receded. Facebook was very much

15 about.instagram.com/blog/announcements/introducing-instagram-stories
16 businessofapps.com/data/instagram-statistics
17 about.fb.com/news/2023/07/introducing-threads-new-app-text-sharing/
18 adexchanger.com/data-privacy-roundup/meta-may-be-rising-from-the-post-att-ashes-but-regulators-still-have-it-in-their-crosshairs/
19 investor.fb.com/investor-news/press-release-details/2024/Meta-Reports-Fourth-Quarter-and-Full-Year-2023-Results-Initiates-Quarterly-Dividend/default.aspx

alive, and the company had found a way to offset, if not completely neutralise, ATT.

Profitability went through the roof. Compared to the previous corresponding quarter, Meta's operating margins had more than doubled from an already impressive 20 percent to an astonishing 41 percent.[20] The effect on the share price was incredible (see Figure 7).

Figure 7: Meta's share price over five years to 2024

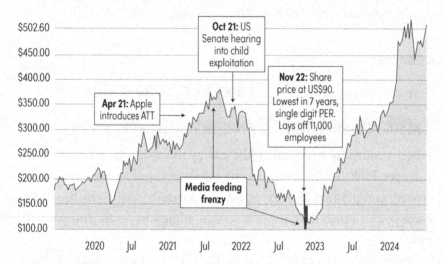

Announcing a 50-cent quarterly dividend and a US$50 billion buyback, the Meta fail narrative was squashed in less than a year. This was now one of the most impressive businesses in the world, an asset-light operating model that was making so much money even Zuckerberg couldn't find much to do with it.

Having predicted this outcome, only one question remained: why didn't I act on Meta, the fattest of fat pitches? I've thought about this but lack a definitive answer, although hindsight bias has pushed me in the direction of finding one. My initial thought was that my analysis of Meta was overly influenced by my personal dislike of Zuckerberg,

---

20 finance.yahoo.com/news/meta-platforms-40-heres-why-110500886.html?

believing that the products he is responsible for are a net negative to humanity. If that were true – and it may be – I should have applied my ethical filter before I spent three months working on it.

The fact that I didn't suggests it is probably an ex-post-rationalisation, which is to say hindsight bias combined with a dollop of self-serving convenience. It is easier for me to accept the 'loss' of a 500 percent gain because I was acting ethically rather being absentminded or surreptitiously exhibiting herd behaviour but unable to own it. I guess I'll never know, and nor does it matter.

Lessons

Here are the lessons we learned from not investing in Meta.

1. Media feeding frenzies provide opportunities

When a company becomes public enemy number one, it pays to take a deeper look. Under attack from regulators, politicians, consumer groups, competitors and advertisers, a narrative had formed, with a share price to match, that Meta was an ailing, desperate company. It wasn't true.

Businesses are complex, as are the environments in which they operate. This complexity is rarely understood and hardly ever properly communicated. Like the dualistic and primitive storytelling of a 1950s cowboy movie, the narrative is superficial. Diamonds can be found if you're prepared to dig into a company's accounts and competitive position to challenge it.

2. Nothing is risk-free

There's a saying in investing that you can't buy a dog without fleas. Companies trade cheaply because of the perceived risks attached to them. TikTok *might* have undermined Instagram, politicians *may* have passed laws that damaged Meta's growth and the company *might* not have found a way around ATT. Those risks were real, and some remain. Meta was a dog with fleas, but the risks were not only incorporated in the price, they were also overstated.

3. Great opportunities are painful

Humans are herd animals. We struggle out on our own in unfamiliar territory. Successful investing asks us to become comfortable with that feeling. Putting money into a publicly castigated stock is painful because it entails going against the crowd. It demands that you understand the consensus and then depart from it. Pain is a result of doing so.

It is not, however, always a sign of being right. The crowd has its wisdom, too. Instead, pain is a sign of following the correct process. You will not get the right result every time, but the greater the pain you feel, the greater the chance of an exciting opportunity.

4. Learn to let go

There are enough fat pitches in an investing lifetime for you to miss a few and still do well. The past is the past. Find a way of learning from it and move on.

Aftermath

Meta is now seen as what it always has been: a hugely profitable advertising business that could be run from Mark Zuckerberg's yacht with a few key employees below deck. The sharemarket is constantly churning out new possibilities. There will be more fat pitches. You may just have to wait a few years to spot one.

Case Study #11
Afterpay

Who wants a 10,000 percent gain anyway?

A human's greatest fear is to look stupid. The best way of overcoming that fear is to confront it. Missing out on Afterpay – a near hundred bagger in less than five years – and not regretting it for a moment is our (very public) contribution.

What happened

If Meta was the company the media attacked like a pack of hungry hounds, Afterpay was patted and petted into the public domain by docile journos enamoured of its technology, youthful audience and global ambition.

Only a handful of companies have breached Australia's geographic distance and small market size to become global successes. Even fewer are technology companies. Atlassian is one, providing software for developers and project managers. WiseTech is another. Neither are household names. Afterpay was different, a technology company for normies who went shopping.

Over the last 40 years, the western world has become substantially richer. This wealth has not been shared equally, including in Australia: real wages have grown minimally or not at all. For capitalism – or, more precisely, its titans – this is a problem. In a system sustained by consumption but plagued by low wages growth and income inequality, how do you get ordinary people to spend money they haven't got, or at least not got yet?

Lay-by was the old-fashioned method. Customers would put a little away each month before saving enough to take the purchase home. That fell out of favour with the advent of credit cards. These offered interest-free periods followed by usurious interest rates for those who met the minimum monthly payment, and scandalous late fees for those who did not.

It is an exaggeration to say that Visa and Mastercard have kept the wheels of capitalism turning whilst making billions each year doing so, but only a slight one. Among merchants and customers, these global brands, much like Australia's Big Four banks, have also become as widely loathed as they are wildly profitable. For consumers, the moaning made little difference. They had no other choice.

That changed in October 2014 when Sydneysider Nick Molnar and his then neighbour Anthony Eisen founded Afterpay.

Afterpay was like a digital lay-by scheme. It took the best bits of the credit card – the convenience of a short-term loan widely accepted by merchants – and excised its more repulsive features, including annual fees, usurious rates, intrusive forms and credit checks. Making a purchase in four easy, interest-free payments, either online or in-store, was as simple as downloading an app. The company's first tagline, 'There's nothing to pay', captured the simplicity.

Millennials jumped at it. In its first few years, Afterpay acquired 1.8 million users[1], and it spent about $100,000 doing so. These are remarkable figures, a testament to the product's appeal. By December

1   abc.net.au/news/2018-05-01/afterpay-instant-interest-free-too-good-to-be-true/9710946

2018, about 4 percent of Australians used Afterpay. Four years later, that figure had more than tripled.[2] Most were millennial credit card refugees happy to sing Afterpay's praises to their online friends. With a brilliantly simple business model, Afterpay had reversed the natural order of things: it had found a way for customers to sell it.

Such was the company's growth and popularity, it listed on the ASX within two years, raising $25 million in an initial public offer (IPO). After floating at $1.00 a share in May 2016, valuing the company at $140 million, Afterpay became a media darling. Then it ascended to verb status.

The credit card industry felt its success. According to data from the Reserve Bank of Australia[3], by mid-2017 Australia had over 24 million credit cards in issue. By mid-2023 that figure had fallen by about a quarter. Afterpay, and the copycats that followed, accounted for most of the decline. The buy now pay later (BNPL) sector was up and running.

Having conquered user acquisition, Afterpay's primary marketing challenge was to expand its network of merchants. This appeared a stretch. The company charged retailers a commission of about 4 percent on every transaction[4], more than that levied by the credit card overlords. In a marketing masterstroke, the company asked users to call their favourite retailer if they did not accept Afterpay and suggest they do. It worked, but only because of a second factor: the transaction commission Afterpay charged could only be justified by an increase in the value of average basket size. If Afterpay could help retailers sell more items or higher-priced items, or both, they might accept it.

The research bore the theory out. In 2015, Afterpay signed its first retail customer: fashion chain Princess Polly. With a customer base too young for credit cards, Princess Polly found that the average

---

2   https://www.roymorgan.com/findings/apple-pay-overtook-afterpay-in-average-users-in-2023-
     to-become-the-third-most-widely-used-digital-payment-service#
3   https://www.money.com.au/credit-cards/credit-card-statistics
4   gocardless.com/en-au/guides/posts/is-afterpay-good-for-business/

basket size of online orders using Afterpay was $44 higher than for those using PayPal. The company ascribed a 15 percent increase in total online revenue directly to Afterpay's adoption.[5] A 2019 report from Accenture found retailers reporting an almost 8 percent revenue increase when partnering with Afterpay.

In May 2018, Afterpay launched in the United States with retailers such as Anthropologie, Free People and Urban Outfitters. Later that year, before Black Friday, Kim Kardashian posted to her 120 million Instagram followers that the family shop now accepted Afterpay. In January 2021, Afterpay reported basket sizes of its US retailers increased by 30 percent during the holiday period. That year, Accenture found US customers saved up to US$459 million in fees by avoiding credit cards and using BNPL, while generating US$8.2 billion in additional sales for merchants.[6]

The merchants were convinced, and if they weren't, seeing their competitors adopt Afterpay swung the argument. With basket sizes and overall sales increasing, the 4 percent commission was a genuine no-brainer.

Afterpay had won, and Molnar and Eisen's vision had been realised. Two years after launching in the United States, it had acquired 5 million users. As of mid-2023, Australian users totalled 3.5 million.[7] The company now operates across the English-speaking world and the European Union.

In 2019, with an estimated wealth of just under $500 million each, the Afterpay founders made their first appearance on the *Financial Review Rich List*.

In August 2021, US company Block, formerly Square, made an all-scrip offer – shares were exchanged rather than cash – for the

5   https://www.afr.com/companies/financial-services/key-moments-in-the-afterpay-story-from-zero-to-39b-20210802-p58f6n

6   https://www.prnewswire.com/news-releases/afterpay-customers-save-up-to-459-million-in-fees-by-not-using-credit-cards---drives-8-2-billion-in-incremental-sales-for-merchants-in-2021--301392798.html

7   https://www.startupdaily.net/topic/fintech/afterpays-australian-users-have-flatlined-as-apple-pay-continues-to-soar/

company. The effective price was $126.21 per share. Molnar and Eisen became instant billionaires.

Afterpay shareholders, including Molnar and Eisen and those who purchased stock in the float, made a 12,600 percent return on their investment, a 127 bagger. When the deal finalised in early 2022, enthusiasm had waned, but those investors still made almost 100 times their money. Few had seen anything like it.

Why it happened

Enviously, we watched Afterpay's rise every step of the way, first publishing research on it in 2018. That article, 'Is Afterpay the next big thing?', concluded it might be. It also stated that it wasn't the kind of business we wanted to own, at least not at the price it was then trading at.

Here are the reasons why I still believe that to be the case.

1. A business model must be proven before investing

During its listed life, Afterpay never turned a profit. For a rapidly growing business expanding into overseas markets, that makes sense. Whether it is sensible for investors to back it is another matter. Before investing in any company, its business model should be secure and stress-tested.

For a company like Afterpay, which made short-term loans, this is especially true. Companies that lend money can look fine when times are good, and during Afterpay's rise times could not have been better. During COVID-19, online shopping boomed as governments threw around free money and interest rates were near zero. The strength or otherwise of a lender is only tested during a recession, when bad loans are revealed. At the time of writing, Afterpay has never faced one.

2. Competitive marketplaces tend not to produce great businesses

BNPL caught on so quickly that, within a few years, IG Markets produced a guide to the top ten ASX-listed BNPL stocks.[8] Overseas, competition was also increasing. Afterpay may have been the dominant player in a competitive market, but its financials provided scant evidence that it would become highly profitable.

Even after the Block acquisition, this remains the case, although the company does not break out Afterpay's financials. Competitive markets generally do not create highly profitable businesses. So far, there is scant evidence that Afterpay will defy this proposition.

3. Regulators eventually act

At the time of our original research in 2018, Afterpay's net transaction margin was a touch over 2 percent. This is similar to Australian banks. But what the banks earn in a year Afterpay earns in six weeks. Customers were contractually required to repay Afterpay over 56 days, taking its annual net transaction margin to nearly 15 percent. With customers repaying almost twice as fast, annualised returns were almost 30 percent.

Afterpay was getting the returns of a payday lender without disgruntled customers and pesky regulation. The barrier to credit was low, and the potential for charges of predatory lending was high. The threat of regulatory intervention was greater than it looked. Since then, regulators have intervened.

Lessons

Afterpay has no historical precedent. It has not been around long enough to show it can survive cutthroat competition or a recession. No one knows the downside and, with Block's consolidated reporting hiding Afterpay's numbers, we're unlikely to ever know.

---

8   ig.com/au/news-and-trade-ideas/top-7-bnpl-asx-stocks-to-watch-in-2020-200916

Its founders and original shareholders got lucky, getting bought out for a princely sum before the bones of the business had come under pressure. They look like geniuses, but the greats are revealed after they have been tested. Nick Molnar and Anthony Eisen did great things but were not fully tested. That task has been left to Jack Dorsey, Twitter founder and chair and co-founder of Block (and current Block Head, as he irritatingly terms himself). Block's share price has halved since the acquisition was completed in January 2021, and it has fallen by three quarters since it was announced in August 2021.

It is possible, although rare, for a company to return to its original shareholders a 10,000 percent gain and still operate an unproven, untested and unprofitable business model. That is what Afterpay did. It is an exceptional case that tempts people into believing their next investment will be the next Afterpay when it almost certainly won't. There is also the possibility the company's original investors ascribe their incredible luck to personal intelligence and skill. Both are dangerous propositions.

Hundred baggers are a trap into which innocent investors willingly fall. These are the reasons why, perhaps counter-intuitively, chasing remarkable successes like Afterpay is one of the worst things an investor can do.

Here are the lessons from missing out on Afterpay.

1. Buying is easy; hanging in is hard

In the early stages of a company's growth, the risk is in the business. Once that has been tested, the risk tends to shift to the share price. People get overenthusiastic and valuations get silly. Jack Dorsey might offer as evidence his purchase of Afterpay.

Getting a hundred bagger entails hanging on through many market cycles, including when the shares you own hit crazy prices. It also asks the business to meet and surpass the growth expectations that have been ascribed to it. The former is extremely difficult, and the latter is unusual.

Having confidence that growth will eventually catch up with the share price is critical when valuations get stretched. For value investors, that's hard. We like to buy stocks with a margin of safety and sell when there's a margin of risk. Because we're confident in our ability to deploy capital elsewhere, we might sell having made, say, three or four times our money rather than aiming for a hundred bagger, hanging on for dear life and suffering the risk that entails.

2. You may well die wondering

Does it count if you die before a stock you own rises 10,000 percent? I ask because a good percentage of readers are probably too old to get a hundred bagger, myself included. Christopher Mayer's book *100 Baggers: Stocks that Return 100-to-1 and How to Find Them* is based on a survey that found 365 hundred baggers between 1962 and 2014. Thomas Phelps's *100 to 1 in the Stock Market*, covering the years 1932 to 1971, arrived at a similar number. Meyer calculates that it took an average of 26 years for these stocks to become hundred baggers.

Afterpay did it in less than five years. The archetype is the exception. For a company to reach hundred bagger status in five years requires a compound annual growth rate (CAGR) of 151 percent. A company that more than doubles in size in a year is incredibly rare; finding one that does so for five years in a row is like finding an alien spaceship in the garden shed. A company with a more realistic CAGR of 17 percent will take 30 years to become a hundred bagger. If you're searching for the next Afterpay, you may well die before finding it.

3. Get set early, go under quickly

The lesson taken by private equity and early-stage funds isn't lost on hundred bagger thrillseekers: the earlier you get on, the greater your chances of getting there. Buy Afterpay at $1 a share and there's your hundred bagger; buy at $5 and you have to wait until... well, it's too late now.

The risk side of the equation is what's missing from this argument. The earlier you buy a business, the more unknowns there are likely to be. Professional investors are more experienced at assessing risk in early-stage companies and use diversification to manage it. They might, for example, have put a few million into Afterpay prior to listing but were making more bets like it elsewhere. They know most will fail, but they only need one big winner to more than cover their losses.

Retail investors tend not to think like this, concentrating their exposure on just a few or even one early-stage company. That increases the risk of a blow-up and limits the possibility of potential upside. The alternative is to wait a few years until after the company lists and make good use of all the information in the public domain. That might reduce your chances of getting a hundred bagger, but it dramatically reduces the risk.

4. Hundred baggers break the golden rule

It's almost impossible to own a stock that goes up a hundredfold without breaking one of investing's cardinal rules: sensible diversification. The chances are high that the rest of your stocks will not go up at the same rate, which means your portfolio is going to become heavily weighted to a single stock.

You can of course sell down as the percentage increases, retaining an ever-smaller parcel of shares. That way you can maintain sensible diversification and still get a hundred bagger. But it won't be anywhere near as much fun, because your $10,000 investment will turn into a few hundred grand rather than $1 million. I'd argue it is better to do well overall, forgoing the bragging rights of your first hundred bagger and all the risks it entails.

Aftermath

Our track record proves that you don't have to own everything that goes up to do well. We prefer to stick to stocks that we believe give us a decent margin of safety. With Afterpay, there wasn't one. If you are unsure about a stock, best stay away.

Investing requires authenticity. Staying true to one's style and approach makes that easier. Avoiding Afterpay may have limited our returns, but flaying yourself over missing out can lead you away from where you excel. We prefer more deeply researched, less speculative bets, letting compounding do its work. Hundred baggers and the stories that imply you just have to seek in order to find are not that. Ninety-nine times out of 100, a company such as Afterpay will not become a hundred bagger in five years.

If you aim to make 100 times your money, there is a far greater chance you will lose most or all of it. Afterpay is an exception, in the history of investing and as an entrant in this book on investing mistakes. I include it so that you may not be distracted by the prospect of unbelievable gains and focus instead on the more ordinary and achievable, which comes with less risk.

REFERENCES

- 18 May 2018: Is Afterpay the next big thing? (intelligentinvestor.com.au/investment-news/is-afterpay-the-next-big-thing/142623)
- 14 Sep 2020: Afterpay: Bulls and bears (intelligentinvestor.com.au/investment-news/afterpay-bulls-and-bears/148633)
- 6 Aug 2021: How we missed Afterpay (intelligentinvestor.com.au/investment-news/how-we-missed-afterpay/150223)

Key takeaways from the stocks we should have bought but didn't

In the 1976 movie *The Gumball Rally*, Franco is preparing for the start of the race. Ripping the rear-view mirror from the windscreen, he cites the first rule of Italian driving to his co-driver: 'What's-a behind me is not important'.

Franco was right. What's behind you does not matter. There will be stocks you almost bought that went on to rise substantially. Assess the reasons for missing out, but do not dwell on what might have been.

Missing a few big winners is an escort to a path that avoids over-paying. It is a means of managing risk. Learn to let go of the ones that got away by thinking of the mistakes they prevented rather than the gains you might have made.

Reflecting on errors of omission is valuable, particularly recognising the pile-on effect and the opportunities it delivers. Media frenzies like the one surrounding Meta cause investors to panic sell. The firestorm *is* the opportunity. It is not risk-free.

Companies trade cheaply because of the perceived risks they carry. Sometimes, those risks eventuate; occasionally, they are overblown and do not. The best opportunities are the most psychologically demanding. Run towards the fire, feel the heat of the flames and calmly decide to either walk away or enter the building.

Embarking on a quest to make a hundred times your money is a terrible idea. Big winners take decades to mature. Afterpay is the exception that proves the rule. Your children, rather than your portfolio, are the likely beneficiaries. Their inattention and disinterest may help you (posthumously) get there.

There is a better way. Select a few well-researched, high-quality investments, purchase them at reasonable prices and let compounding do its work. By not seeking, you may find.

Appendix

This appendix contains seven essays that go deeper into the issues raised by the case studies on which this book focuses. Each has been lightly edited since its original date of publishing. The first two concern business models. Through an examination of the historical development of the music industry, 'Can't buy me business models' explains aggregation theory and how the Internet has created a new kind of monopoly. Amazon, discussed in 'Roundabouts and flying wheels', is a good example. Using Jim Collins's flywheel effect, it shows how, once established, innovation, growth and higher profitability spin at an ever-faster rate. The contrast with poor models such as Timbercorp, PMP and Amaysim could not be more stark or more useful.

Without exceptional management, no business will capitalise on the benefits of an outstanding business model. With crooked, incompetent or fraudulent management, investors are likely to do poorly no matter what. 'Red flags and avoiding disaster' identifies the behavioural and practical red flags of a business going off the rails.

'Why breaking up is hard to do' examines the psychological factors that make buying and selling stocks difficult and suggests techniques, developed from bitter experience, to improve them.

You must first buy a stock before you can make one of the errors described in this book. 'How to feel the fear and buy anyway' examines the buying decision and explains why the harder it feels, the more likely it is that you are doing the right thing. 'Making better decisions' is a useful follow-up, addressing how to improve your environment and structure your day in a way that makes higher-quality decisions more likely.

Investing, I believe, demands an inherently optimistic view of the world, conditioned by localised pessimism. This isn't easy. The world has its problems, we are predisposed to catastrophise, and humans tend to adopt a short-term view. But if you don't believe the future will be better than the past, there is no point investing at all. With a long enough time frame, there's good reason to believe it will be. 'The case for optimism' looks at what our species has achieved over a few hundred thousand years as a reminder of that fact.

Can't buy me business models

First published 9 June 2017

The Internet has totally revolutionised how business is done. There are important lessons for investors and music buffs alike.

'Guitar groups are on their way out, Mr Epstein.' With those words, Dick Rowe of Decca Records turned down The Beatles. Well, supposedly. Rowe denied saying them till his last breath, but history charged him anyway.

What few people understand is that Rowe wasn't an outlier. Every major label on both sides of the Atlantic repeated his error without it making one iota of difference to their long-term wellbeing. The record companies operated a business model made in a sky with diamonds. If you missed a few stars, well, it didn't matter.

For many Londoners, Liverpool remains a distant, provincial city, reached by a nightmarish train trip from Euston to Lime Street, which perhaps explains why Dick Rowe sent his assistant to The Cavern. They were evidently impressed. Nineteen days later, after a ten-hour drive in a snowstorm, The Beatles auditioned for Decca.

It did not go well. In *Anthology*, McCartney admits 'we weren't that good', although Lennon, contrary to the last, said, 'We were just doing a demo. They should have seen our potential'. Had Liverpool been closer to London, Rowe might have. Instead, he signed The Tremeloes, from Dagenham, Essex, a reasonable cab ride from his Hampstead office.

The Beatles were turned down by six major UK labels, including EMI, before George Martin signed them to EMI-owned Parlophone in 1962. The story of missed opportunity then made its way across the Atlantic. On 4 April, 1964, The Beatles occupied the top five spots in the Billboard charts, courtesy of four different labels. EMI's US label, Capitol Records, had just two of what might have been five giant hits. How so? Capitol saw the UK as a musical backwater. The US had invented rock and roll and the Yanks weren't about to be pushed around by a country that last topped the US charts with Acker Bilk, a trad jazz clarinet player from Somerset who had lost half a finger in a sledging accident.

EMI didn't push it. Instead, it banged on the industry's biggest doors and got knocked back. Only after three independent labels took a flyer on the unknown UK outfit did Capitol capitulate. Had George Martin not been around, an entire industry may have missed the biggest act of all time. The illustration of aggregation theory in Figure 8 explains why.

There are three components to any value chain: suppliers, distributors and consumers. Prior to the Internet, the best way to maximise profits was to operate a monopoly as a supplier or distributor, forcing one party to deal with another. The other option of so-called vertical integration was to integrate two of the three parts of the value chain.

Record labels were and still are an example. In controlling the artists but also the production, marketing and distribution, labels integrated supply with distribution. Newspapers and publishers did similarly. Through people like Dick Rowe, the labels were the gatekeepers.

Without a recording contract, bands had nowhere to go. It was the model that was the haymaker, not a particular group that passed through it. As if to prove the point, a few months after missing out on The Beatles, Rowe signed The Rolling Stones. One of the advantages of controlling the value chain is being able to wait for the next bus.

Figure 8: Aggregation theory

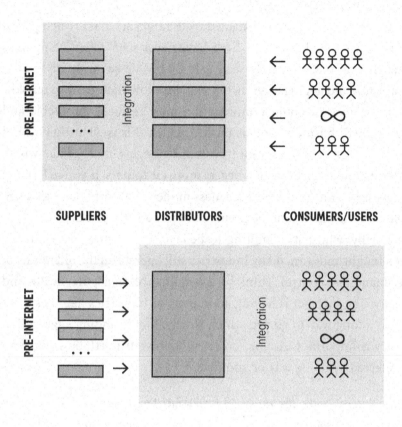

The second part of diagram explains the departure from this model, a point lost on many investors. Once a product like a music track, book or advertisement can be digitised, the cost of distributing it falls to zero. This generally shifts the power and profits in the value chain away from suppliers and distributors towards those who can aggregate demand, which is to say consumers.

Once the Internet captured the attention of everyone, powering the growth of businesses like Facebook and Google, newspapers were cooked. Free-to-air television is suffering a similar, albeit slower, demise due to the same causes. The same goes for taxis, video stores, travel agents, electrical retail chains and, really, any category that Amazon has entered.

Customer aggregation, enabled by the Internet, has created global monopolies the likes of which we have never seen. Giant companies now grow at rates formerly seen only by businesses with far smaller footprints, and aggregation theory explains how they grow so quickly.

If an investor could nominate the most resilient, profitable and high-growth business models on the planet, this is what they would look like, especially as more customers begets more data, which begets better services, which begets more customers. If you're looking to invest in some of the best business models the world has ever seen, well, join the queue, and be prepared to pay a hefty price.

Finally, whilst it's tempting to believe these battles have already been fought and won, many industries still operate on the old model of command and control. Think banking, finance, transport, health and energy. The Internet is having an impact on industries like these, but there's a long way to go yet, which is why understanding aggregation theory is important. Almost every stock in your portfolio is likely to be affected by it one way or another.

Coda: Interestingly, the music industry has fared better in the Internet era than newspapers and book publishers. Apple's iTunes aggregated customers by focusing on user experience, weakening the label's grip on distribution, as aggregation theory indicates. But they retained control over supply. Then, the arrival of streaming services like Spotify, Amazon Music and Tidal opened more distribution channels, reducing Apple's dominance. It's not as good as it was back in Rowe's day, but it could have been worse.

Roundabouts and flying wheels

First published 29 November 2019

You may think investors have little to learn from the UK Roundabout Appreciation Society. I beg to differ.

In 2001, someone scrawled a drawing on a napkin that proposed a way Amazon could conquer the world. As a metaphor for how it did so, I propose a roundabout 80 miles west of London – all this, you understand, in the search for attractive, growing businesses that might one day acquire monopoly characteristics.

Identifying existing monopolies is as easy as stepping out the door. If you wish to fly from Melbourne to Sydney and then drive to the Hills district, ambitiously aiming to arrive the same day, Sydney Airport and Transurban's M2 are unavoidable. So are either Virgin or Qantas. If you want to buy their shares on the way, add an ASX toll to the list.

Then there are sectors dominated by a handful of companies, none of them technically monopolistic but collectively behaving as one. These are typified by poor products and low levels of customer satisfaction. With few or no alternatives beyond the cartel, these companies can facilitate terrorism and child abuse, pay billions in fines and still make money hand over fist. Yes, I'm talking of the banks, of course.

If purchased at attractive prices (a hefty caveat), both kinds of monopolies offer shareholders the prospect of handsome returns. But neither are likely to match the profits of an immature but quickly growing business that might one day establish a monopoly of its own. These businesses can drive portfolio returns from above average to astounding.

What has been lacking is a framework to support that task. The objective here is to put that right. As Charlie Munger said, 'You can't really know anything if you just remember isolated facts and try and bang 'em back. If the facts don't hang together on a latticework of theory, you don't have them in a usable form'.

Munger's mental models, from the circle of competence and thought experiments to inversions and probabilistic thinking, offer a systematic way of interpreting the world and thinking more intelligently about it. I'd like to add roundabouts – or flywheels, to use Jim Collins's description – to the list.

Everyone is familiar with roundabouts and their ability to accelerate traffic flow. Good businesses, like roundabouts, have at their core an accelerating momentum that just seems to work.

At the age of 26, Jeff Bezos joined hedge fund D. E. Shaw, specialising in potential online investments. Having made a list of 20 products he thought could be sold online, Bezos landed on books as the most viable. His superiors knocked back his idea, and so, in 1994, he left to start Amazon.

The customer proposition was simple: deliver to customers a larger range of books at lower prices than competitors. That got the business going. Then, in 2001 at an Amazon shindig, Bezos codified the strategy on a napkin. The company has abided by it ever since. Figure 9 shows Amazon's model in a nutshell.

Everything starts (and ends) with customer experience. A huge selection of books made possible by the Internet, lower prices made possible by the absence of stores and a focus on volume, plus an easy-to-use website, made Amazon irresistible. Booklovers came in their droves.

Figure 9: Amazon's flywheel

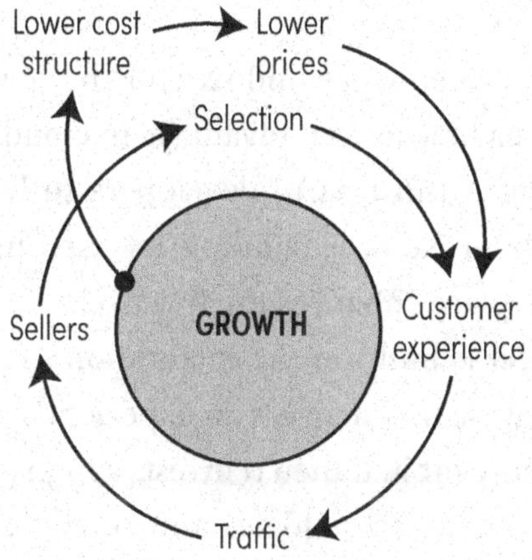

SOURCE: SAM SEELY, THE AMAZON FLYWHEEL: PART 1

In aggregating demand, Amazon then opened its platform to third-party sellers of just about everything. Keen to access Amazon's extraordinary traffic, their growing presence created more competition, which lowered prices and increased the range of available products, which attracted more customers. The costs of servicing each customer could then be spread over an ever-growing number, reducing marginal costs.

In *Good to Great*, Jim Collins called this the 'flywheel effect'. Once spinning, a business develops a momentum of its own. In Amazon's case, as long as management remained focused on customer experience – wider choice, quicker delivery, lower prices – the business would continue to grow no matter what.

The flywheel effect has another advantage. In feeding energy back into the business and increasing its growth velocity, management is free to innovate and experiment without sacrificing growth. You may giggle at Amazon's Fire Phone or Google Wave, but the same motivations that led to these hilarious failures also delivered Amazon Web Services, Amazon Prime, Google Chrome and Android. A flywheel encourages businesses to take risks and to fail occasionally without losing focus.

The purpose is to enhance and extend the flywheel effect. Xero, having established a first-mover advantage in cloud-based accounting software, encouraged third-party developers to build products that would integrate with Xero, expanding its usefulness to customers. Xero's App Marketplace enhances the flywheel.

Apple's flywheel is built on the integration of superior hardware with bespoke software that delivers an experience users love so much they can charge more for it. It then reinvests a high proportion of those growing profits in new technologies and supply chain management to expand the flywheel, delivering more products and services that enhance the ecosystem. Cochlear's flywheel looks much the same (see Figure 10).

Figure 10: Apple (and Cochlear's) flywheel

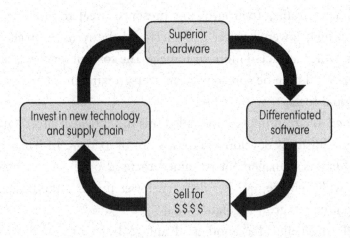

SOURCE: STRATECHERY.COM

148

Once a business has established a flywheel and recognises how to maximise its impact, higher research and development (R&D) often ensues. This alone is not enough. Without an understanding of the flywheel, further investment can be misdirected. The same might be said of acquisitions.

The flywheel is a conceptual tool to help you recognise and understand high-quality growth businesses. The next step might be to re-examine some research and see whether you can create a flywheel for each. If so, sketch out what form it takes. From personal experience, there is no better way of getting a bird's-eye view of a company and what makes it tick.

If you find the process difficult, either your understanding of the business is not yet fully formed or the flywheel is weak or non-existent. Both are valuable perspectives.

Conventional analysts prefer to trawl through annual reports, industry research and ASX announcements, tinkering with a spreadsheet as they go. These things are important, but without an understanding of the business and how it connects with the customer in the real world, assembled facts and data points carry little meaning. A flywheel offers a framework through which facts and events can be interpreted.

And so to Swindon, an unremarkable UK town with a Magic Roundabout. In 2007, *Auto Express* magazine named it as one of the world's worst junctions, largely because it features multiple round-abouts in one (see Figure 11, overleaf).

The Magic Roundabout is a perfect metaphor for how the likes of Google, Amazon and Alibaba have built multiple flywheels around the central proposition that Jeff Bezos landed on all those years ago. It is this that allows some of the world's biggest businesses, decades after their founding, to still grow revenue at astonishing rates.

These are the portfolio makers – the one or two stocks that can turn your prospective retirement from cat food to caviar. Swindon's Magic Roundabout might just help you to spot them sooner than everyone else.

Figure 11: Swindon's Magic Roundabout

Red flags and avoiding disaster

First published 6 June 2016

There are many signals that should keep you out of certain stocks. These are the big ones.

Some years back, some *Intelligent Investor* analysts returned from an AGM slack-jawed and bewildered. The meeting, they said, had a cultish, messianic tone, more revival gathering than sombre report to shareholders. One analyst thought there was a better-than-even chance of a fraud. Another said the company had the 'most promotional management' he had ever seen.

Intrigued, I set off to read the transcript. Neither claim seemed hyperbolic. Further digging supported the initial impression. In 2012, the chief executive was paid a salary of US$420,000. Stock awards and options pushed total remuneration over US$6 million. That same year, the company generated US$5.52 million in revenue.

Softly ringing in the background were more alarm bells. In a former life the CEO had sold 'investment analysis software'. *The Sydney Morning Herald* reported in 2004 that he owned two Mercedes and a Bentley Continental GT, once clocked doing 231 km/h on the way to Canberra for a purported meeting with the Prime Minister. Neither is conclusive, but from such events an unflattering picture emerges.

In 2006, the newly floated company's CEO was sued by an ex-lover. During the case, a barrister claimed the company's largest shareholder, a Roger Williamson, was in fact an alias for the CEO. Then, in 2009, the company left Australia to list on the Nasdaq, whereupon the CEO's brother was recruited as a senior vice president. Shortly before listing, the company announced target revenues of US$400 million by 2014. The inaccuracy of that forecast was pinpoint.

There aren't many cases of a CEO's remuneration exceeding the annual revenue of the company under their management. Alan Shortall, for that is who he is, CEO of retractable syringe company Unilife, managed it in 2012 and came close two years earlier.

At least the love was shared. In 2015, three executives received packages of over US$1 million. In a year when revenue reached US$13.2 million, the combined remuneration of the six top executives hit US$13.8 million. Board fees added almost another US$1 million. Everyone appeared to be in on the game.

The losses mounted and the debt grew. In the U.S. Securities and Exchange Commission (SEC) 10-K form for financial year 2013, the US equivalent of an Australian annual report, the auditors said the company had 'incurred recurring losses from operations and has limited cash resources, which raise substantial doubt about its ability to continue as a going concern'. In March 2014, chief financial officer Richard Wieland resigned without taking up another appointment.

Through more debt and regular capital raisings, Unilife continued. Despite its obvious problems, Jefferies, the company's broker, would issue buy recommendations on Unilife and then raise capital for it, urging investors to have 'continued patience'. The result was constant and horrendous dilution. Short-seller Kerrisdale Capital reckoned that a shareholder from 2006 would have suffered an 83 percent dilution by 2013.

In 2013 Talbot Smith, a former Unilife employee turned whistleblower, accused the company of fraud and SEC rule violations. The SEC had its own reason to apply scrutiny.

In March 2014, Unilife had secured a loan from OrbiMed. In an unconventional move, the SEC had granted the company confidential treatment of the loan's covenants. Shareholders were not to know its details. Two months later, Stone Street Advisors lodged a freedom of information request, claiming that 'investors cannot assess when/if Unilife is or will be in technical default without this information'.

Although the request was denied, pressure was mounting. The company fought back, urging the SEC to rein in the malicious short-sellers, one of whom may have been famed value investor Whitney Tilson. In one email to Jefferies, Tilson asked, 'At what point are you going to wake up and stop being snookered by a master con man????' It was as if the CEO's very name was a harbinger.

Soon after, everyone did wake up. In early 2014, Unilife share-holder Cambridge Retirement System filed suit over 'excessive and wasteful' compensation. Despite winning an EY Entrepreneur of the Year™ Award, in March 2016 Alan Shortall resigned as CEO, taking a lump sum cash payment of $420,000. Chief operating officer Ramin Mojdeh also departed. In May, the company fell foul of Nasdaq listing rules in its failure to file a 10-Q and announced that its third-quarter earnings call would be delayed. Then a class action against the company was announced.

For shareholders, it was all too late. On 27 April 2010, Unilife hit $1.31 a share. It closed in early June 2016 at 8 cents. Aside from Unilife's management, broker and board, the only people to have profited from the adventure were short-sellers. For over a decade, more red flags were flying over the company than a 1960s communist rally, but somehow it endured.

The human brain is predisposed to choose facts and opinions that make sense of the past. It would be easy to see Unilife in this light, an obvious disaster in waiting. But there is always a counterargument.

Despite the claims of Tilson and others, no proof of fraud has ever emerged. As for the whistleblower, he withdrew his claims, apologised and paid an undisclosed amount to the company.

Unilife may have been a management enrichment vehicle, but that is not illegal. (The case brought by Cambridge Retirement Systems was dropped, too.) Nor is repeatedly demonstrating the gullibility of investors and the compromised nature of brokers.

Moreover, Unilife was no paper tiger. In 2016, when Shortall was still CEO, OrbiMed stumped up another US$10 million in debt financing and Amgen injected US$50 million into the business in return for access to the company's product portfolio.

When examining the history of this stock – one screaming trouble for years – what seems clear-cut now wasn't quite so obvious at the time. This is not to say there was ever a case to view Unilife favourably, but it does highlight the problems inherent in a 'red flags' approach to avoiding future losers.

Whilst avoiding speculative stocks like Unilife will reduce your chances of a blow-up, it also means missing out on big winners. And if excessive CEO pay is a red flag, well, where can you invest these days?

Even in a disaster-in-waiting like Unilife, there exists a seductive grey area into which our desire to see things work is naturally drawn. Without an established product pipeline and new management, to say nothing of a reasonable price, this injection syringe maker was a company we could never recommend.

The reason for choosing it as our 'red flags' example was not because of the ease of spotting them but to show how easy they are to miss, even in situations as conclusive as this.

It would be simple to assume investors caught up in the crash were stupid or foolish, but that would be unfair. If avoiding stocks like Unilife were merely a question of pulling out a checklist and ticking a few boxes, the *Intelligent Investor*'s recommendations history would be almost error-free, and clearly it isn't.

More importantly, the best opportunities tend to be difficult to buy, which is why one person's red flag is sometimes another's good fortune. If you want to buy cheap stocks, you're going to have to deal with a few warts. Avoiding them is a question of their kind and number.

Table 1 groups red flags into behavioural and practical categories, with the latter frequently an expression of the former. A fish, as they say, rots from the head. Unilife featured many of these unwelcome behaviours, but there are more.

Table 1: Red flags

Behavioural	Practical
· Talking the share price up	· Remuneration incentives
· Litigious	· Aggressive accounting
· Key staff leaving in quick	· Related-party transactions
succession	· Lack of industry experience on
· Nepotism	board
· A love of jargon	· Poor board attendance
· Hero-style leadership	· Diworsification / global ambitions
· Corporate extravagance	· Little board investment in
· CEO also chair	business

Behaviour like this is more common among smaller companies, where founders or large, private shareholders can dominate the register. With less scrutiny, there's more scope for self-enrichment. The issue is one of representation. In theory, a company is owned and run by management for the benefit of shareholders. In practice, some companies are run for the benefit of management at the expense of shareholders.

Management theorists call this an 'agency problem', and nowhere is it more colourfully expressed than at Disney circa 1997. Chief executive and chairman Michael Eisner's grip on the company was so absolute that the 17-member board featured Eisner's personal attorney, his child's school principal and Sidney Poitier.

The California Public Employees' Retirement System (CalPERS) has developed a three-point test to establish whether a board is independent or not:

1. It must have a majority of independent directors.
2. The chair must be one of them and not also act as CEO.

3. The compensation and audit committees must be exclusively composed of outsiders.

In 1997, Disney was the only S&P 500 company to fail on all three measures.

When a CEO's grip on a business is so tight, the checks and balances on decision-making are whittled away. Behavioural red flags eventually turn into practical warning signs. Arrogance and self-regard ultimately lead to a host of other problems, from nepotism and extravagance to a stacked board, disgruntled employees and grandiose expansion plans. When ego takes over, it is shareholders who pay the price.

This takes us into different territory. Unilife featured a ludicrously compensated CEO and a board and senior executive team that was paid handsomely, perhaps as a way of keeping them sweet. Although this is a bad sign, it is not a conclusive predictor of a poor outcome.

Egregious salaries are tolerable if they accrue from activity that also benefits shareholders. Unfortunately, in many cases they don't. Misalignment of remuneration with shareholders' interests is a major warning sign. And remunerating managers on share price performance is not alignment, merely an incentive to talk share prices up and underinvest in a business.

There is nothing absolute in the spotting of red flags, no conclusive waving that screams 'avoid'. One way of dealing with this complexity and the natural human bias to optimism is to list all of the factors that concern you and then make the counterargument. List each point side by side to see how the arguments weigh up. Instead of applying fixed rules and jumping to conclusions, in this way we force ourselves to consider all relevant facts more deeply.

One final point. There will be cases where, despite ill-conceived management incentives and behavioural red flags, companies will do well. We do not need to invest in these businesses for our portfolios to perform well. We can afford to be cautious, avoiding companies that might not pass the smell test but where nothing is rotten. We don't have to be invested in every stock that goes up to do well. Be fussy.

Why breaking up is hard to do

First published 15 May 2017

Why selling a stock is more difficult than buying it and what to do to make it easier.

ARB, featured in Part II: Stocks We Sold Too Soon, was one of my better performers, but over the years I regularly felt the urge to sell. When the global financial crisis (GFC) hit, I presumed a decline in non-discretionary expenditures was inevitable. Twelve-volt fridge freezers for four-wheel drives were surely the epitome of that description. Didn't happen. Nor did the collapse in commodity prices that might have caused a fall in demand for ARB's products targeted at the sector.

Then there was the fact that my investment had first doubled, then tripled, then quadrupled. That old saying about not going broke taking a profit jumped into my head each time. I could say I was wise enough to resist, but that's not true either.

The real reason is that life – children, health scares, divorce… the usual stuff – got in the way, and, after six years with *Intelligent Investor*, I needed a break. That enforced inactivity worked in my favour. The result was an accidental five bagger.

Buying stocks is easy, or at least it can feel that way. Developing analytical skills is simply a matter of time and application. Most of us can get reasonably good at it. Then, once we find an undervalued stock, excitement and overconfidence kick in right before we hit the 'buy' button.

If approached sensibly, the act of building a portfolio should make us more astute buyers. The selling decision, on the other hand, entails us overcoming more psychological factors than inherent optimism. The problem can be split between rising and falling share prices, and selling too early or too late. Let's deal with selling early first.

Note: in the following headings, the word 'good' refers not just to the quality of a business but also the degree of discrepancy between its price and intrinsic value.

1. Being too quick to sell a good stock after its price has risen

If we believe that we 'can't go broke taking a profit' it's easy to sell too early, denying us the opportunity to allow a good stock to compound returns over time. This reveals the human bias towards activity, regardless of its consequences, over inactivity. There's a reason why 'Just do it' resonates with so many of us.

For many investors, the act of trading is what shrinks might call a 'self-actualising moment', where the act of buying or selling a stock brings their own ideas about themselves to life. To not trade therefore becomes a denial of self.

2. Hanging onto a poor stock after its price has risen

In ARB's case, the rise in its stock price was accompanied by a commensurate increase in intrinsic value. But what about a situation where it isn't, where a stock's price is rising without good reason? This decision is equally complicated but for different reasons. The act of doing well in a stock makes us more psychologically committed to it, which makes selling harder. This is part endowment effect – where people ascribe more value to things merely because they own them – and part fear of missing out (FOMO). If the mere act of receiving something creates value, as research suggests, imagine the impact of paying for it and then seeing its price rise?

More behavioural heuristics kick in. Recency bias encourages us to conclude that recent price rises indicate future price rises. And FOMO ensures we hang on to take advantage of them, even though they may not happen. Then, heaven forbid, if the share price does continue to rise, these effects are compounded by confirmation bias – the tendency to interpret new evidence as confirmation of one's existing beliefs or theories. No wonder selling a stock with a rising share price is hard.

3. Being too quick to sell a good stock after its price has fallen

If anything, for investors facing a tumbling share price it's even worse. First, we are prone to conclude that a share price fall is evidence of a problem. (It sometimes is, although only in hindsight is this revealed.)

Again, this is loss aversion. We may have lost, say, 30 percent of our stake, but that exacerbates concerns about hanging on to the remaining 70 percent. Even if further analysis reveals the magnitude of the share price fall is out of proportion to the underlying problem, we can be 'panicked out'.

4. Hanging onto a poor stock after its price has fallen

Sometimes a share price fall *is* warranted, and we fail to appreciate the change in circumstances. New information that departs from the original investment case can lead a company away from where we expected and hoped it might be. The endowment effect slows down this realisation, leading us to hang on longer than we should.

Concentrating on the price we pay for a stock makes good sense, but it's only the first leg of a three-legged stool that supports a good trade, from the initial purchase to the final sell.

The second leg hits the ground at the same time as the initial purchase. When we buy a stock, we should also establish the mental framework and potential trigger points for evaluating when we might get out. By thinking about selling whilst we're buying, when the time to sell arrives – the third leg of a successful investment – we're more likely to get it right.

*

Here are four simple strategies to improve your chances of getting it right from the start. When buying, ensure you have:

1. **A clear idea of a stock's intrinsic value.** Anchoring can cause investors problems, but in this case it can serve you well. With a good idea of what a stock is worth, your potential exit price becomes clearer. And if the share price falls below intrinsic value, you won't be so easily persuaded to panic. Stay focused on the value, not the price.

2. **A mental picture of the path you expect the business to follow.** Because value changes over time, a roadmap can help. By having a mental picture of where you expect a business to be in a few years' time and the markers it should pass along the way, it's easier to recognise departures from the expected course. If a company surpasses the markers you have in mind for it, as good companies often do, you have less reason to worry, although it's still vital to check on progress. Either way, your expected roadmap for a stock is a powerful tool, especially if written down.

3. **A sell target in mind.** Setting a sell target at the point of purchase removes the temptation to hold a stock simply because it is rising. Think of it as the endpoint in your roadmap, but be prepared to adjust it for changes in underlying value.

4. **A maximum portfolio weighting.** The idea of establishing a maximum portfolio weighting at the point of purchase is to focus on how much damage a stock might do in the event of collapse. This can help shift thinking away from company-specific optimism to overall portfolio risk.

Doing these things should set you up to make good decisions about selling, but you'll still have to overcome all the emotional and psychological pitfalls when you get there. Here are some strategies to help improve the sell decision:

1. **Ignore recent price movements.** It's all too easy to sell stocks just because they've fallen for fear of further falls, or to hang on to those that have risen in the expectation of further rises. When a stock seems to be on a charge, it's tempting to hang on for a little longer. There's nothing to suppose a stock that has risen will rise some more, or that a falling stock will fall more. Momentum is an illusion, something that is there until it is not. Decide what's the best thing to do at any given price, ignoring recent price movements.

2. **Use tranche selling.** Buying and selling in stages can make it easier to deal with price movements by leaving room to buy more of a stock that's fallen (assuming the investment case is still on track), and conversely, by selling portions of stocks that have risen. This will keep your portfolio weighting in check and help to overcome the attachment to a stock that seems to be rising.

3. **Imagine your portfolio is 100 percent cash.** Another good way to overcome attachment is to pretend you don't own any stocks at all. You can then ask yourself whether the set of stocks before you, at their current portfolio weightings and prices, is what your portfolio would look like if you had to start over. This won't eliminate the endowment effect, but it can help overcome commitment to past decisions.

4. **If that doesn't work, sell anyway and consider buying back.** If pretending you don't own a stock doesn't work for you, there's a more radical approach – sell it and then consider whether you'd be happy to buy it back at the same price. Value investors aim to minimise transaction costs, and this technique increases them, which is why the practice isn't widespread. But by selling a stock

and perhaps waiting a while before deciding whether you want to own it at current prices, you escape many of the psychological traps selling sets. It might be worth the brokerage.

5. **Revisit the original investment case.** Having a roadmap for each stock you own can help to understand whether a company you own has departed from the reasons why you originally purchased it, and if so, how far. In May 2015, for example, we confessed that our original investment case for SMS Management wasn't working out. The move into managed services was going okay, but it was the promise of a return of high-margin consulting work that had drawn us to it. When that failed to materialise, we sold. The stock proceeded to fall a further 60 percent. Without checking the original roadmap, we may have held on longer than we should have.

6. **Use the broken thesis test.** The commitment principle makes it hard to reverse a decision because it increases our tendency to look for information that confirms a view and overlook facts that might contradict it. If you think the investment case has changed but you're still hanging on, it's probably a sign that your psychology is making you do it. The lesson is to sell a stock where you've potentially made a mistake before it becomes one.

How to feel the fear and buy anyway

First published 11 August 2011

'One broker (The Clown of Collins St) came in yesterday saying "Capitulation over ... now's the time to buy ... expect a short-term rally of 3–4%". Dickhead. Typical of the "guess, guess and guess again" value add of some financial professionals.'

Marcus Padley, *Crikey*, 9 August 2011

As things transpired, the dickhead was right. A few hours after those words were published, the ASX All Ordinaries index had risen not 3 or 4 percent but 5. Whether stocks are rising rapidly or crashing, the market makes fools of us all.

Value investors implicitly understand that cheap stocks are a product of pervasive fear just as expensive stocks are an expression of greed. But in both cases, when the time comes to act, many of us stumble.

Often, it's not our value investing skills that fail us but our psychology. What follows is a dose of psychological fortitude to help you avoid critical mistakes and profit from the opportunities in collapsing share prices.

1. Hold cash and ensure it's quickly accessible

Affording you the ability to act quickly, cash is not a dead asset. When prices are cheap and opportunities plentiful, cash is the source of future returns. If you haven't accumulated much of it during the good times, take some tough decisions. Don't hold stocks in your portfolio just because they've been there for years when better opportunities exist outside it.

Ensure that cash is not stuck in a three-month term deposit or requires an overnight bank transfer before you can use it. It should be available through your broking account at a moment's notice.

2. Have a watch list with buy prices

A watch list is a great technique to sideline emotions that can prevent you from acting. If you know what you want to buy and at what price, you'll be more likely to act when the time comes.

Developing a watch list gets the commitment principle working in your favour, especially if you show the list to friends or display it in a prominent place so you get social proof working for you as well.

3. Prepare an action plan; buy gradually

Now you've got the cash and an idea of what you want to buy at a particular price and yield, you need an action plan. This technique relies on you committing to a course of action before gut-wrenching emotion takes over.

Do not pile in all at once. Buy gradually, acquiring more shares as prices fall. Buying at the point of maximum pessimism is a great ideal but impossible to confidently execute without the benefit of hindsight. Buying gradually in fearful times and sticking to high-quality companies at prices cheap enough to offer a good margin of safety is a more realistic aim.

4. Stick to portfolio limits

There's every chance that a few of the stocks in your portfolio won't work out as you expect. That is the nature of investing. The damage these failures might do to a highly concentrated portfolio won't be fatal to a more diversified, well-structured one.

As in many areas of life, we need to stay alive long enough to get lucky. Don't kill your portfolio by loading it up with a few highly speculative stocks. Concentrate on the high-quality businesses and diversify, paying close attention to portfolio limits.

5. Challenge your evolutionary impulses and buy anyway

We're programmed to respond to fear because in the past it was a successful way of not being eaten. In the sharemarket, fear inhibits rational, profitable action.

*

Whilst these practical steps help you to act when the time comes, we also need to reassert a few fundamental investing truths that conflict with our typical reactions to uncertainty and rapid share price falls:

- **If you want certainty, you're going to have to pay for it.** When everything's going well, you won't get anything cheap. Bargains are a product of a climate of fear. If you want to buy cheap stocks, you must feel the fear and buy anyway.

- **Accept that prices may fall after you've bought.** You can't pick market bottoms or tops, but if you're buying high-quality businesses cheaply, that shouldn't stop you from buying more when prices fall further.

- **Separate price falls from underlying business performance.** The market can be irrational. To avoid getting caught by the herd, focus on business performance, not macro issues (important as they may be) or media headlines. This is the major, long-term determinant of share price direction.

Making better decisions

First published 14 October 2015

The brain is wired to undermine portfolio performance, but there are ways to bypass the malfunctioning.

About 200,000 years ago an early Homo sapiens emerged from his cave, pulled on a woolly mammoth cardigan and fired up the Nespresso machine. Looking out over the Great Rift Valley with his morning brew, he felt the burden of familiarity. The valley had become as crowded and noisy as hippos and giraffes had become scarce. It was time to go for a long walk.

A few billion people later, Homo sapiens, by then a success of plague proportions, underwent another transformation, this time academic rather than geographic.

Kickstarted by John Stuart Mill in the 19th century, Homo economicus emerged fully formed a century later when Lionel Robbins's rational choice theory took the economics profession by storm. Man, it was thought, was largely rational, a maximising utility machine driven by self-interest, a dollar-hunter supreme.

Homo economicus made the study of economics a predictable affair. With an entirely rational subject, theories could be easily advanced, models simply constructed and the results analysed much in the way of physics or mathematics.

Economics moved from the humanistic base established by the likes of Adam Smith and Edmund Burke to a more mechanistic practice. Sociologists scoffed at the idea of rational decision-making, but our universities were stuffed with people whose careers depended on its maintenance. Only with the 1979 publication of *Prospect Theory: An Analysis of Decision Under Risk*, did Homo economicus come under sustained attack.

Amos Tversky and Daniel Kahneman, the book's authors, offered evidence of human irrationality, of decisions made for reasons other than self-interest. Over the last few decades, irrefutable evidence has emerged to support their conclusions. Humans are a weird, unpredictable, model-breaking mob.

If we are to improve investment decisions, we first need to know *how* our brain makes them.

Let's take an example. Linda is 31, single, outspoken and bright. She majored in philosophy. As a student, she was deeply concerned with issues of discrimination and social justice, and participated in anti-nuclear demonstrations. Rank in order of likelihood these scenarios – Linda is:

1. an elementary school teacher
2. active in the feminist movement
3. a bank teller
4. an insurance salesperson
5. a bank teller also active in the feminist movement.

Now, you and I both know that (5) cannot be more likely than (3), but a 1983 study by Tversky and Kahneman indicated that a bewildering 85 percent of respondents thought it was. The researchers believe this was due to our brains seeking out cause – in this case literally – and effect at the expense of calculating probability.

Another example is based on a study of eight parole judges in Israel. Each spent entire days reviewing applications, presented in random order, with an average of six minutes spent on each case. The research recorded the overall number of requests approved, the time of each decision and when the judges took their three food breaks.

The researchers then plotted the proportion of approved requests against the time since the last food break and found that about 65 percent of requests were granted after each food break. During the two hours or so until the judges' next feed, the approval rate dropped steadily, hitting zero just before the next meal.

You don't need to believe that judges are food-obsessed tyrants to accept these findings, only that denying parole is their default position, that departing from it requires intellectual effort and that such effort depends on circumstance.

Behavioural psychologists are challenging the concept of Homo economicus, replacing the concept of the brain as a device for making rational decisions with something more complex and confusing: a machine for jumping to conclusions, a muscle that gets tired and reverts to the status quo, and the source of different forms of thinking for different situations.

One of Tversky and Kahneman's key insights was that the brain is subject to what psychologists call 'dual process theory', an unconscious, automatic way of taking decisions (system one thinking) and another that is explicitly conscious and controlled (system two).

As Kahneman wrote in *Scientific American*:

> When we think of ourselves, we identify with System 2, the conscious, reasoning self that has beliefs, makes choices, and decides what to think about and what to do. Although System 2 believes itself to be where the action is, the automatic System 1 is the hero of the book.

This is a problem for investors. We like to think we're rational, that we're taking decisions whether to buy or sell a stock having undertaken a cold review of the facts. In truth, we're often using system one, acting emotionally and instinctively but kidding ourselves system two is doing all the work. Our Israeli parole judges, who were happy to employ system two thinking after a rest and some food but reverted to system one as their energy and attention waned, offer a real-life example of how this plays out.

The challenge, then, is in getting our brains to adopt system two thinking when just about everything around us – panicking investors, screaming newspapers headlines, crashing stock prices, Jim Cramer – send us into an emotional state that makes system two thinking all but impossible.

Perhaps the best place to start is to ensure you're in the right frame of mind to make decisions in the first place.

1. Decide what's important

Decision-making is undermined by the number of decisions the world asks us to make. The more we decide, the less capable we become at taking the next decision. Like a muscle, our brains tire.

The first, important decision of your day, therefore, should be to decide what your biggest, most important decisions are. Make a list if you want to. It may be a portfolio review, a choice about whether to sell a stock, or which review of a stock on your buy list to follow up. In writing them down or mentally noting them, accept that everything else is peripheral and can be easily dispensed with.

2. Decide early in the day

Allocating time to the most important decisions at the beginning of the day means you're more likely to be refreshed and undistracted, which increases the chances of high-quality system two thinking.

Getting irritating decisions out of the way first – what to eat for dinner; who's going to fix the toaster – is energy-depleting. Don't sweat the small stuff. Leave it until later in the day, after you've taken your most important decisions.

3. Create a distraction-free environment

If your home is stacked with devices like tablets and mobiles phones, allowing you to check email in the toilet or update your Facebook status in the bath, your environment works against good decision-making. Making good decisions requires concentration. Get these devices out of the room, turn off the computer, grab a pen and paper, find a comfy chair, sit back and just think.

4. Reduce your decisions

A longer-term strategy is to reduce the number of decisions you have to make each day. Instead of having to think about what to cook for dinner, have a weekly menu plan. Instead of wondering if you have enough time to visit the gym, develop a weekly routine so you know what you'll be doing day to day. For decades, Warren Buffett has dined at Gorat's Steak House in Omaha, ordering much the same thing each visit. This is oddly repetitive but means he has two less decisions to make each time he goes out to eat.

5. Don't just do it, start on it

The problem with the Nike slogan 'Just do it' is that when we don't just do something, we feel bad about it, which makes just doing it next time even harder. The solution is not to wait but to start. Getting started is like a miracle cure for procrastination and muddled thinking, enabling a mental state that usually overcomes what has been blocking us.

Set yourself the goal of starting something, not finishing, and rely on the mindset of being fully absorbed in an activity to get you to the finish line.

6. Write it down

The best way to see if you really understand an argument is to write it down as if you were telling someone else. This is known as the 'Feynman Technique', named after the Nobel-Prize-winning physicist. High-performing investors also know the benefits of writing things down. As Mortimer Adler, author of *How to Read a Book*, once wrote, 'The person who says he knows what he thinks but cannot express it usually does not know what he thinks'.

Before buying or selling a stock, write down your reasons for acting first. If you find the task difficult, chances are you aren't clear in your mind about why you're acting.

7. Multi-tasking is rubbish

Stanford University's Anthony Wagner claims that multi-taskers are 'not able to filter out what's not relevant to their current goal' and that this failure means 'they're slowed down by that irrelevant information'.

Even worse, University College London found that multi-tasking with electronic media had an effect on decision-making worse than smoking marijuana. Turn off your phone, avoid email and concentrate on the task at hand. If you're going to stuff something up, do you really want two screw-ups for the price of one?

8. Take a break, say 'no' and focus on what's important

Most of the decisions you take today won't have a bearing on the quality of your life in five years' time. Investing decisions will. All too often we neglect decisions that impact our future because we want to be superficially appreciated. That's why we find it hard to say 'no'.

People might not like you for it, but it's best not to sweat the small stuff. Give yourself plenty of mental space to make the big decisions. Learn to say 'no' to people, focus on what's important, and when you get tired, take a break so that you can return to tasks at hand refreshed.

9. Don't beat yourself up when you're wrong

Just because you've made a commitment to improve your decision-making doesn't mean all future decisions will be good. To get better at things, first we must fail. Accept it, learn from it and move on.

The case for optimism

First published 8 December 2017

There's no point investing if you don't believe the future will be better than the past. If your time frame is long enough, there's good reason for believing it will be.

Living deep in the outer suburbs of West London, my grandmother spoke fondly of World War II. On hearing the air raid sirens she would run to the garden, waiting for the sky to turn 'dark with bombers', to use the words of Billy Bragg.

Banks of Spitfires and Hurricanes would rise to meet them, buzzing her house, filling her with pride. Despite living through the postwar glory days when work was plentiful and housing cheap, later in life, whilst reflecting on one of humanity's greatest destructive acts, she found happiness.

She was not alone in twisting memory to revere the past. We all do it. How else to explain my parental belief that every child can be improved by a paper round, vinyl records and a gobstopper? As David Hume wrote in 1777, 'The humour of blaming the present, and admiring the past, is strongly rooted in human nature'.

He has a point. Implicit in a glorified past is a pessimistic future. But there is a strong case for optimism, not just in an economic and investing sense but in the general trajectory of human history. We may have our challenges, but we should not underestimate our capacity to meet them.

About 1.8 million years ago, the Acheulean hand axe was peak technology, the Swiss Army Knife of its millennia. Developed 3.5 million years ago, the hand axe was around about 1.5 million years before the use of fire by Homo erectus, and long before Homo sapiens (us) displaced Neanderthals about 200,000 years ago.

Only with the arrival of the Greeks, Romans and various Chinese and Middle Eastern dynasties did the pace of change begin to accelerate, at which point the axe fell on the hand axe. Then, around the middle of the 17th century, something remarkable happened.

Figure 12: Historical life expectancy in various countries

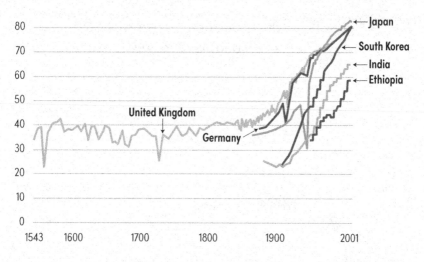

Around 1550, average life expectancy in the UK was about 39 years. It stayed that way for 300 years but by 1850 began to rise. Within 200 years it had more than doubled. The reason was the Industrial Revolution, which began around 1760, the effects of which took some time to spread.

Figure 12 covers some significant history. The Renaissance began in about 1400, when science as a means of understanding the world began to usurp religion. It took a mere 300 years before scientific inquiry led to the kind of inventions that made the Industrial Revolution possible – water, steam and coal power, the telegraph and the diesel engine. All put a Stephenson's Rocket under economic growth.

The link between growth and life expectancy is hinted at in the experience of South Korea. A century ago, the average Korean lived a mere 27 years. After rapid industrialisation, life expectancy tripled. A similar process is now underway in India, China and other developing nations.

It's a remarkable transformation. For hundreds of thousands of years human life barely changed. Then, in the last 200, it changed beyond all recognition. Triggered by the revolution, economic growth is the reason for it. How's this for correlation (see Figure 13).

Figure 13: US life expectancy versus real GDP per capita (log) 1929 to 2010

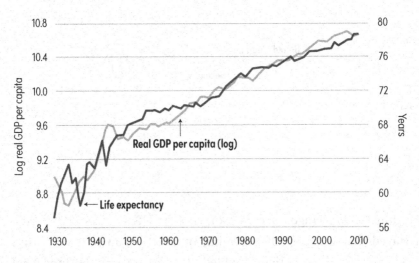

All kinds of inventions have made this possible. Economist Tim Harford's book *Fifty Inventions that Shaped the Modern Economy* nominates, among other things, shipping containers, concrete, the barcode, antibiotics, insurance and IKEA's Billy bookcase (you'll have to read it to understand why). Each has allowed us to sustain an ever-larger population living ever-longer lives.

Nothing better illustrates the magnitude of human progress than the declining cost of artificial light. In the language of MasterChef, this was the game-changing immunity pin (or maybe vaccination was). Anyway, instead of sleeping or shagging in the dark, people could learn, build, think, invent, draw and write in the light.

Bill Nordhaus, a Yale economist, became obsessed with the subject, trawling through the scant economic data to establish the historical cost of man-made light. He discovered that during the Babylonian period one day's average wages could purchase a mere ten minutes of light, generated from a primitive oil lamp.

It stayed that way for 4,000 years, until 1850 in fact, when a Canadian discovered how to get kerosene from coal and oil. A day's wages now purchased about five hours of light. The next breakthrough was the big one, Edison's original lightbulb moment about 30 years later. At the time of the Nordhaus study in the 1990s, a day's labour bought 20,000 hours of cleaner, instant, reliable electric light.

We may moan about our electricity bill, but at least we don't have to catch a whale to get enough oil to read the microwave instructions on a TV dinner (which, incidentally, made it into Harford's top 50). Man-made light was once too precious to use. Now it's so cheap we barely think of the price, and when we do we install solar panels. Instant, cheap light has led to a huge increase in productivity and human invention.

The upshot of all this is that it's far better to have an ordinary income now than to be extremely rich 100 years ago, watching your kids die of polio while the maid empties the chamber pot, dreaming of boiled tripe. That, quite literally, is progress. So, why the pessimism?

I'd propose three reasons, although there are probably more. The first concerns our many psychological biases, starting with the availability heuristic. Take the media's infatuation with shark attacks, house fires, bombings and car crashes – known as the 'if it bleeds, it leads' approach. Anything memorable we deem more likely to occur, which is why many of us believe crime is at record highs (it's near record lows) and Muslims are more prone to engage in terrorism (they're not).

The second explanation concerns our evolutionary wiring and attitude to risk. The cost of under-reacting to the threat of being eaten by a lion was potentially a lost life. The cost of overreacting is only a missed meal. This made sense 100,000 years ago – now, not so much. We still overreact to threats because the wiring in our brains has not caught up with our changed circumstances.

The third is our limited capacity to imagine life beyond our own experience of it. Our brains see time through the prism of our own lives. That makes grasping the full, historical extent of human existence difficult, causing us to miss the lessons it offers.

This is not to argue humanity has a clear run to the future. There are obvious and serious challenges, but greed, stupidity, narcissism, selfishness, arrogance and conceit have always been with us.

But look at how far we've come in just 200 years. The silicon chip has changed our lives already but was only invented in 1961, genes can now be edited, and artificial intelligence and machine learning offer enormous promise, to say nothing of the inventions to come. Even your Christmas turkey this year will be twice the size of what it was 50 years ago.

Along with many others, I've experienced the pace of progress in an intimate and beneficial way. In 2003, I was diagnosed with leukaemia. According to the stats, my life expectancy was eight years. Immunotherapy now means I'll probably live to an average age, without factoring in future advances.

So, I'm looking to the future, the one just over the horizon. We may not be around to see it, but in another 200 years my guess is humanity will look back on today as my grandmother did – venerating the past whilst failing to see how far we've come and what we've achieved.

Glossary

All Ordinaries: The oldest index of shares in Australia, comprised of the 500 largest companies listed on the Australian Securities Exchange (ASX).

ASX 200: A sharemarket index comprised of the 200 largest and most liquid companies listed on the Australian Securities Exchange (ASX).

Australian Securities Exchange (ASX): Australia's primary securities exchange.

Average revenue per user (ARPU): A measure of the amount of revenue generated on average from each user of a service, calculated by dividing total revenue by the total number of users.

Big Four: The four main banks in Australia – ANZ, Commonwealth Bank, NAB and Westpac.

Capex (capital expenditure): Money spent by a company in acquiring, maintaining and upgrading its assets.

Capital raising: A process through which a company raises funds from external sources to achieve its strategic goals.

Cash flow: Money being transferred into and out of a business. *See also 'discounted cash flow', 'free cash flow' and 'operating cash flow margin'.*

Commitment bias: The tendency to remain committed to past behaviours even if they do not have desirable outcomes.

Competitive advantage: The factors or characteristics that put a company in a favourable position with respect to its industry peers. *See also 'moat'.*

Compound annual growth rate (CAGR): The (geometric) average annual rate of growth over a period in something, such as revenue, or profit, or a share price.

Confirmation bias: The tendency to interpret new evidence as confirmation of existing beliefs.

Day trading: The buying and selling of shares over a period of a single day, with the intention of profiting from small price fluctuations.

Discounted cash flow (DCF): A method of estimating the value of an investment by discounting its expected future cash flows back to today's value. *See also 'cash flow'.*

Dividends: Sums of money paid regularly by a company to its shareholders out of its profits.

Diworsification: The process by which a company acquires other companies or assets beyond its core business in order to broaden its revenue sources, but often diminishing its overall quality.

EBIT (earnings before interest and tax): The measure of a company's profits before interest expenses and taxes are deducted, often used as a measure of *operating profit. See also 'EBITDA'.*

EBITDA (earnings before interest, tax, depreciation and amortisation): *EBIT*, but also excluding depreciation and amortisation, thus attempting to represent the cash profit generated by the company's operations.

Free cash flow: The cash that a company generates after cash outflows. *See also 'cash flow'.*

Gearing: Calculated in a number of ways, but intended to show how much debt a company owes compared to its equity. *See also 'net gearing'.*

Gold rush effect: A situation where expected future demand outstrips supply.

Hundred bagger: A stock whose value has increased to 100 times your initial purchase price. *See also 'ten bagger'.*

Initial public offering (IPO): The process of offering shares in a company to the public for purchase.

Insider buying: The purchase of shares in a company by someone within the company.

Intrinsic value: The perceived or calculated value of an investment. *See also 'margin of safety' and 'value investing'.*

Leverage: The borrowing of funds to finance an investment. *See also 'operating leverage'.*

Loss maker: A product, company or industry that consistently fails to make a profit.

Margin of safety: The gap between the market price of an investment and its *intrinsic value.*

Market capitalisation: A company's sharemarket value, calculated by multiplying the total number of its shares by its share price.

Mergers and acquisitions (M&As): The consolidation of companies or their major assets.

Moat: A company's ability to maintain its *competitive advantage.*

Narrative bias: The tendency to interpret information as being part of a larger story or pattern, whether or not the facts support this.

Non-renounceable rights issue: A *rights issue* where the right of existing shareholders to subscribe for new shares cannot be sold and traded.

Operating cash flow margin: A measure of a business's cash from operating activities as a percentage of sales revenue over a given period. *See also 'cash flow'.*

Operating leverage: A measure of how revenue growth translates to growth in *operating profit*, used to calculate a company's break-even point and help set selling prices. *See also 'leverage'.*

Operating Profit: The profit generated by a business unit, excluding how it is financed and how it is taxed. *See also 'EBIT'.*

Outflow: Money flowing out of a company; expenditure.

Price earnings ratio (PER): The measure of a company's share price relative to its per-share earnings, often used to put some context to the price of a company's shares (and to help decide whether they are overvalued or undervalued).

Redundancy: The intentional duplication of critical functions, which increases reliability.

Return on equity: A company's net income divided by its *shareholders' equity*, which can be used as an indication of the company's profitability.

Return on investment: *Yield* plus the change in the market price of a security held by an investor.

Rights issue: When existing shareholders are offered the opportunity to purchase more shares in a company, pro rata to their existing holdings. *See also 'non-renounceable rights issue'.*

S&P 500: A sharemarket index comprised of the 500 largest companies listed on stock exchanges in the United States.

Same-store sales: A measure of the growth in revenue from store locations that have been in operation for at least one year.

Scrip: A substitute for legal tender (such as shares), entitling the bearer to receive something in return.

S-curve (sigmoid curve): The typical shape of a graph showing the progress of something over time, featuring a slow start, followed by a sharp rise and then a levelling out.

Shareholders' equity (or 'equity'): The funds contributed to a company by shareholders, through the issuance of shares and the retention of profits. *See also 'return on equity'.*

Sovereign risk: The risk that a foreign government will default on its bonds or impose foreign exchange regulations.

Specialty retailers: Stores that focus on specific product categories.

Store growth: A measure of the increase in store locations.

Tail spend: Ad hoc, uncategorised spending that is low in volume, frequency or value.

Ten bagger: A stock whose value has increased to ten times your initial purchase price. *See also 'hundred bagger'.*

Value chain: The progression of activities that a group of companies engage in to deliver goods or services to customers.

Value investing: An investment strategy that involves picking stocks that appear to be trading for less than their *intrinsic value*, thereby providing a margin of safety.

Yield: The annual payments an investor receives for owning an investment, typically in the form of interest (on cash or bonds), rent (on properties) or dividends (on shares). *See also 'return on investment'.*

Acknowledgements

This book is a result of the contributions, directly or otherwise, from a host of people who have passed through the doors of *Intelligent investor* over the last quarter-century. In that sense, it is a collective effort. My job has been to first record and then analyse our experiences, often with the aid of their recollections. Some of those people deserve special mention.

Without Robert Carey, who co-founded *Intelligent Investor* along with me, it would never have got off the ground. Special mention also goes to Greg Hoffman, Steven Johnson, Gareth Brown, Nathan Bell, Gaurav Sodhi, Graham Witcomb, James Carlisle and James Greenhalgh, all of whom played important roles in establishing and developing our value investing culture and approach. Their contributions were essential in achieving our performance track record and building a loyal, intelligent and participatory membership. If you have ever read *Intelligent Investor*, you too have played a part.

James Carlisle deserves special mention. His incredible recall, command of the English language and forensic eye helped knock the book into shape. I'd also like to thank my partner Tuty Juhari, whose total lack of interest in investing encouraged me to make each case study jargon-free and easily understood.

Back in 1998 when we started, I could scarcely have believed I would be working in the same field a quarter of a century later. The fact that I am still enjoying doing so is equally improbable. My colleagues listed above, plus recent additions Nick Cummings and Angus

Donohoo, are responsible for making the work interesting and fun. I am grateful for their company, intelligence and collegiate approach.

Lastly, I'd like to thank my publisher at Major Street, Lesley Williams. Without her urging, patience and direction, it is unlikely this book would have been started, let alone finished. I apologise for the delays.

About the author

Intelligent Investor founder John Addis has a long-standing fascination with investing and what makes good businesses tick. He's written for the *Sydney Morning Herald* and *The Age* and, for reasons still unknown, studied economics at university. He is also a founding partner of Private Media, owner of *Crikey* and *The Mandarin*, and a director of online portfolio manager Sharesight.

In his spare time, he takes calls from his three adult children, cooks roast potatoes and feeds his addiction to English Premier League football. He has never had a beard.

Keep in touch with him via:

Website: Intelligentinvestor.com.au
Book: HowNottoLose1Million.com

**Be better with
business books**

MAJOR STREET

We hope you enjoy reading this book. We'd love you to post
a review on social media or your favourite bookseller site.
Please include the hashtag #majorstreetpublishing.

Major Street Publishing specialises in business, leadership,
personal finance and motivational non-fiction books. If you'd
like to receive regular updates about new Major Street books,
email info@majorstreet.com.au and ask to be added to our
mailing list.

Visit majorstreet.com.au to find out more about our books
(print, audio and ebooks) and authors, read reviews and find
links to our Your Next Read podcast.

We'd love you to follow us on social media.

in linkedin.com/company/major-street-publishing
f   facebook.com/MajorStreetPublishing
⊙   instagram.com/majorstreetpublishing
𝕏   @MajorStreetPub